Poor for the Poor

The Mission of the Church

Cardinal Gerhard Müller

Foreword by Pope Francis

With the Writings of Gustavo Gutierrez and Josef Sayer

Libreria Editrice Vaticana
United States Conference of Catholic Bishops
Washington, DC

Contents

Foreword

Pope Francis

Who among us does not feel uncomfortable when even simply confronting the word "poverty"? There are so many forms of poverty: physical, economic, spiritual, social, and moral. Above all, the Western world identifies poverty as the absence of economic power and negatively emphasizes this status. The Western world's government, in fact, is founded essentially on the enormous power that money has acquired today, a power that is apparently superior to any other power. Therefore, an absence of economic power signifies irrelevance on the political, social, and even human level. Whoever does not possess money comes to be considered only according to the measure in which he or she can serve other purposes. There are many forms of poverty, but economic poverty is the one that is regarded with the greatest horror.

There is a great truth in this. Money is an instrument that in some way—like property—prolongs and increases the capacity for human freedom, giving the ability to work, to act, and to bear fruit in the world. In and of itself money is a good instrument, as are almost all the things that man uses: money is a means that enlarges our possibilities. Nevertheless, this means can be twisted against man. Money and economic power, in fact, can be a means that distances man from man, confining him in an egocentric and egotistical horizon.

The same Aramaic word that Jesus uses in the Gospel—*mammona*, that is a hidden treasure (see Mt 6:24; Lk 16:13)—makes us understand that when economic power is an instrument that produces treasures that one keeps only for oneself, hiding them from others, it produces iniquity and loses its original positive value. The Greek term, used by St. Paul in the Letter to the Philippians (see Phil 2:6)—*harpagmos*—also refers to a good that is maintained jealously for oneself, or even refers to the fruit of that which is stolen from others. This occurs when goods are utilized by one who knows solidarity only through the group, be it small or large, of one's own acquaintances or when one seeks to receive solidarity, but not when one seeks to offer it. This happens when man, having lost hope in a transcendent horizon, has lost also the taste for gratuity, the taste for doing good for the simple beauty of doing it (see Lk 6:33ff.).

When instead man is educated to recognize the fundamental solidarity that binds him to all other men—the social doctrine of the Church reminds us—then he knows well that he cannot keep for himself the goods which are at his disposal. When he lives habitually in solidarity, man knows that what he denies to others and keeps for himself, sooner or later, will be turned against him. In effect, Jesus alludes to this in the Gospel, when he highlights that decay or moth ruins riches possessed egotistically (see Mt 6:19–20; Lk 12:33).

Instead, when the goods at one's disposal are utilized not only for one's own needs but are also spread abroad, they multiply and often bear unexpected fruit. In fact, there is an original link between profit and solidarity, a fecund reciprocity between gain and gift, which sin tends to break and obfuscate. The task of Christians is to rediscover, to live, and to proclaim to all this precious and original unity between profit and solidarity. How much does the contemporary world need to rediscover this beautiful truth! The more the contemporary world consents to do its financial books with this, the more it will diminish the economic poverty that so much afflicts us.

Therefore, we cannot forget that not only economic poverty exists. It is Jesus who reminds us of this fact, warning us that our life does not depend only "on our goods" (see Lk 12:15). At our origin, man is poor, needy, and indigent. When we are born, in order to live, we need the care of our parents, and thus in every age and at every stage of life, none of us will ever succeed in freeing ourselves totally from the need and help of others; no one will ever succeed in removing from himself the limit of impotence before someone or something. This is also a condition that characterizes our status as "creatures": we are not made by ourselves, and by ourselves we cannot give ourselves all that we need. The honest recognition of this truth invites us to remain humble and to practice solidarity with courage, as a virtue indispensable to life itself.

In every instance, we depend on someone or something. We can live this as a weakness of life or as a possibility: as a resource for rendering accounts with a world in which no one can do without the other, in which we are all useful and precious for everyone, each in his own way. There is no way to discover what moves us toward a responsible and responsive praxis, in view of a good that is then truly both personal and common in an inseparable way. It is evident that this praxis can come about only from a new mentality, from the conversion to a new way of looking at one another! Only when man sees himself, not as a world standing apart, but as one who by his nature is linked to everyone else, feeling toward them all like a "brother" from the first, is a social praxis possible in which the common good does not remain an empty and abstract word!

When man envisions himself thus and is educated to live accordingly, the original creaturely poverty is no longer felt as a "handicap" but as a resource, in which what enriches each person and is freely given is a good and a gift that later redounds to the advantage of everyone. This is the positive light with which the Gospel also invites us to look at poverty. It is especially this light that therefore helps us understand why Jesus transforms this condition into an authentic "beatitude": "Blessed are you who are poor!" (Lk 6:20).

Then, although doing everything that is in our power and rejecting every form of irresponsible tolerance of one's own weaknesses, we do not fear to recognize ourselves as needy and incapable of giving ourselves everything we need, because by ourselves and with our own strength we cannot succeed in overcoming every limitation. Let us not fear this recognition, because God himself, in Jesus, has bent down (see Phil 2:8) and continues to bend over us and our poverty to help us and to give us those goods which, by ourselves, we can never have.

Therefore, Jesus praises "the poor in spirit" (Mt 5:3), that is to say, those who look to their own needs, and being needy as they are, entrust themselves to God, not fearing to depend on him (see

Mt 6:26). From God we can in fact have that good that no limit can stop, because he is more powerful than every limit and this he proved to us when he conquered death! God as one who was rich became poor (see 2 Cor 8:9), in order to enrich us with his gifts! He loves us; every fiber of our being is dear to him; in his eyes each one of us is unique and has an immense value: "Even the hairs of your head have all been counted. . . . You are worth more than many sparrows" (Lk 12:7).

I am therefore grateful to His Eminence, Cardinal Gerhard Ludwig Müller, Prefect of the Congregation for the Doctrine of the Faith, that with this present book he has wanted to remind us of all of this. I am certain that each one of us who will read these pages will, in some way, allow his heart to be touched and will feel rise up within himself the demand for a renewal of life. Therefore, dear readers, know that in this exigency, and on this road, you find me even now with you, as a brother and a sincere companion along the way.

Franciscus

The Liberating Mission of the Church

I. The Word of God and the Signs of the Times

I had a very concrete experience of the Church that is poor for the poor in Peru, in the slums of Lima and among the citizens of the Andes, astonished when, encountering those people, I saw and perceived a faith full of joy and life. The faith witnessed to openly and transmitted with love is among the greatest treasures of these peoples, although weighed down by enormous daily preoccupations for their own life: "Blessed are you who are poor, for the kingdom of God is yours" (Lk 6:20).

But for me the Church that is poor for the poor also has the face of Gustavo Gutierrez. Permit me therefore to offer some introductory words about the importance of my experience in Latin America and on the significance of my friendship with Gutierrez; and not only with respect to my understanding of the ecclesial and theological movement known as the theology of liberation—as it is thus defined by him in his writings—but also for the development of my own theological reflection, in particular on the theme of the love of the Church of Jesus Christ for the poor.

Twenty-five years have passed already since Joseph Sayer—for many years rector of Misereor—invited me, together with other German and Austrian theologians, to participate in a seminar on the theology of liberation, directed by Professor Gustavo Gutierrez and held near the famous Bartolomé de las Casas Institute in Lima, Peru.

It was 1988 when I was called to take over the chair of dogmatic theology at the Ludwig Maximilian University of Munich; and since I had delved more deeply into the works of the exponents of that current of Catholic theology, the great documents were familiar to me to which this theology was referring: those conciliar and post-conciliar documents, as also the Declarations of the second and third general assemblies of the Latin American episcopate at Medellín and Puebla. I was inside the debate that the theology of liberation had caused, and I knew quite well the two "Instructions" of the Congregation for the Doctrine of the Faith regarding it: *Libertatis Nuntius* of 1984 and *Libertatis Conscientia* of 1986, both signed by the then-Prefect, Cardinal Joseph Ratzinger.

Now, the personal encounter with Gustavo Gutierrez revealed itself as particularly fecund for me, precisely on account of the full maturation of an understanding of that which is a theology that goes beyond a single dimension: that is to say, "passive" and "theoretical," scientific and academic.

During this sojourn in Lima, we also spent some time together in the slums on the outskirts of the city, with the least of the least, and afterwards with the *campesinos* of the parish of Diego Irarrazaval, near Lake Titicaca. We witnessed those whom the brigands of today—people blinded by avarice and without pity—had struck and robbed, taken advantage of and oppressed, reduced to near death, and abandoned, bloody, on the roads of the world: people whom mercy alone would have been able to save, the mercy of someone who, on account of love, would have stopped there, bending over them.

From that time forward, during the many times that I returned to Latin America and, above all, to Peru—usually taking advantage of the months of the summer break from academic activity—my participation in the theological courses or seminars always went side by side with long weeks of pastoral service, which took place for the most part in the regions of the Andes, mainly in Lares, in the Archdiocese of Cuzco. In this way, taking as the starting point the concrete experience of nearness to those for whom Gutierrez had developed liberation theology, that which represented the heart of liberation theology was becoming always clearer to my eyes: its heart is an encounter with Jesus; it is to follow Jesus Christ, the Good Samaritan.

This is so because Jesus is not a proclaimer of a mysticism that is detached from every reference to the world, or of a disincarnate asceticism. In the teaching and in the action of Jesus, there is, on the contrary, a unity between the transcendent and imminent dimensions of salvation. Nor can his Death on the Cross in any way be considered as a religiosity detached from the world, separating creation from redemption. Rather, Jesus died on the Cross in order to demonstrate the liberating love of God that transforms the world. Jesus' Death on the Cross conferred on the world and on history the characteristic of a field in which the new creation imposes itself, starting with the here and now. Thus salvation, liberation, in regard to its historical realization, does not begin at the moment of our individual death or at the end of the history of humanity in its complexity, when the Good Samaritan will return: rather, the moment of the fulfillment of it is in the contemplation of God, in the eternal communion of love with him. It begins here and now, on the streets.

From here, there are some acquisitions of liberation theology, as taught by Gustavo Gutierrez, and which it seems to me opportune to underscore, also synthetically.

If, therefore, as has been said, "preferential option for the poor in the last instance is an option for the Kingdom of God that Jesus proclaims to us," as Gutierrez underscored in a conference held in the mid-1990s before, among others, Cardinal Ratzinger, then, he continued, "the definitive reason for involvement with the poor and the oppressed is not the social analysis that we utilize, nor the direct experience that we are able to have of poverty, or in our human compassion. All these things are valid motives that have without a doubt a significant role in life and in solidarity. Nevertheless, inasmuch as we are Christians, this involvement is fundamentally based on faith in the God of Jesus Christ. It is a theocentric and prophetic option that puts down its proper roots in the gratuity of the love of God and is demanded by it."[1]

Jesus Christ died so that man might experience God as salvation and life in all the spheres of existence. Thus, the original impulse of liberation theology emerges: an impulse that is theological. It is not possible to speak of God without active, transforming, and therefore practical participation in the full and integral liberating work

3

inaugurated by Christ, through which history becomes a process in which freedom is effected.

Therefore, if the Church, one with the human race and in history, is at the service of this plan of Christ, then, as Dietrich Bonhoeffer writes, she is able to be the Church only if she is a Church for others. In other words, there emerges a fundamental and unavoidable *aut/aut*; or, to say it with the first, fundamental paragraph of *Gaudium et Spes*, "The joys and the hopes, the griefs and the anxieties of the men of this age, especially those who are poor or in any way afflicted, these are the joys and hopes, the griefs and anxieties of the followers of Christ," or one is not truly a disciple of Jesus: either the Church, from this perspective, presents itself not as a religious community separated from the world and self-sufficient but as the universal sacrament of salvation,[2] or the Church, as regards her nature and mission, is not fully the Church. The Church is truly such if she is faithful to her liberating mission for the integral salvation of the world, which has its origin in the message of freedom and liberation of Jesus and in the very action of Jesus, as affirms the document *Libertatis Conscientia* of 1986 (Chapter IV).

Today, as in the times of Bartolomé de las Casas, God is on the side of the poor and works to bring them to freedom and to grant them participation in the integral action of the salvation of all people, as promised by him. At last, from this perspective, it becomes absolutely clear that, when one speaks of "the historic strength of the poor," this is far from the formulation of an ideology of service of yet another utopian and violent project, as the critics more or less interested in this expression have often affirmed. With "historic strength" of the poor, one certainly does not intend, on the model of Communism, the violent elimination of one social class to be replaced by another, seen as a way to eliminate oppression and injustice and to reach the presumed paradise on earth of a society without classes. The love and action of God embraces also the dominators, those who take advantage, liberating them from their own slavery: that slavery typical of avarice, of the idolatry of money and power, through which one never finds peace. One does not ever have enough: one always wants more, and one is always possessed by the restlessness of having to seize life for oneself by taking it from others.

But above all, unlike what sustains Marxism, and, to be precise, also today's unbridled capitalism, liberation theology as taught by Gustavo Gutierrez demonstrates precisely how Christianity is not a "consoling ideology." On the contrary, the true, authentic liberation theology demonstrates that in truth only God, Jesus, and the Gospel can have an authentic and lasting role for the humanization of man, whether considered individually or socially. It is, in other words, what St. John Paul II synthesized in his felicitous expression found in the Letter to the Episcopal Conference of Brazil in 1986: Liberation theology, rightly understood, "is not only opportune, but also useful and necessary."

The judgment of St. John Paul II has not lost any of its relevance; rather, it has much more value today. In an era in which hostility and avarice have become super-powers; in an era in which we think we no longer have need of that living God who loved us unto death, that Good Samaritan who, in his unmeasured love, in the fleshiness of concrete existence, bows down toward the suffering, the oppressed, and those in need of salvation; in an era, finally, in which, in the beautiful words of Pope Francis pronounced at Rio de Janeiro July 27, 2013, during the encounter with the Brazilian episcopate: "We need a Church capable of rediscovering the maternal womb of mercy. Without mercy we have little chance nowadays of becoming part of a world of 'wounded' persons in need of understanding, forgiveness, love."

II. Human Development between Creation and Fulfillment: Notes on the Encyclical *Sollicitudo Rei Socialis* of St. John Paul II

An Approach to the Social Doctrine of the Church

The *Compendium of the Social Doctrine of the Church*, published in 2004,[3] is the most recent position of the Church on the vast theme of the social doctrine of the Church and places itself in the long tradition of the attention and care that the Church has for man, and for the social development of man that would do justice to his being and nature. In this sense, the Church has always taken into account all the dimensions of the reality of man, considering herself as a point of permanent reference for a social doctrine oriented toward man, in his particular political or cultural context. At the center is always placed the individual man, in the same way that he, who is by nature in relationship with God, is loved and willed by God.

The necessity of a wider involvement in the sphere of social doctrine in Europe emerged already in the eighteenth and then the nineteenth century. Industrialization and progressive developments in the sphere of technology transformed man himself into a machine: a machine that must serve production unconditionally, to guarantee always greater services and therefore greater profit. Thus, man is relegated to the second place.

Workers, degraded to cheap labor, found in Pope Leo XIII an advocate who knew how to anchor firmly the attention of the Church for the social question to the consciences of individuals and of the entire world. Changes in the economic field in the nineteenth century were at the foundation of the overturning of a centuries-old social order and raised serious questions in the field of justice; at the same time, the first great social questions were arising, such as the question of work that arose in the sphere of the relationship between capital and work itself. The new phase of the processes in the world of work was a stimulus to reflect on the pastoral challenges that, consequently, were changing, so as to confront the new conditions with adequate means. The affirmations of the Magisterium along these lines followed with *Quadragesimo Anno* (1931), *Mater et Magistra* (1961), *Pacem in Terris* (1963), and *Gaudium et Spes* (1965). Three encyclicals of St. John Paul II followed: *Laborem Exercens* (1981), *Sollicitudo Rei Socialis* (1987), and *Centesimus Annus* (1991).

For a True Human Development

The Second Vatican Council forcefully affirmed that "the joys and the hopes, the griefs and the anxieties of the men of this age, especially those who are poor or in any way afflicted, these are the joys and hopes, the griefs and anxieties of the followers of Christ. Indeed, nothing genuinely human fails to raise an echo in their hearts."[4] It is an appeal that precisely today has a burning relevance, since the condition of man in many regions of the world has assumed dimensions and features so alarming as to render urgently necessary the social and charitable work of the Church. They give rise to sorrows and anguish, hunger and misery, conditions of slavery and persecution, even to the murder of masses, which characterize the life of millions and millions of persons around the whole world. Pope Benedict XVI was very aware of it when, with regard to the great challenges of the present and of the future, with the Encyclical *Deus Caritas Est* (2005) he wanted to impress on the consciences of individuals, of states, of nations, and of peoples the unique role of the Church for the building up of a world that is worthy of man.

The Encyclical *Sollicitudo Rei Socialis* takes up again in a particular way the notion of "development," linking it to that of peace. It recalls the hope that *Populorum Progressio* of 1967 had for movement toward conditions for a more humane life, characterized by not only purely technical and economic dimensions, but also a development in the sphere of culture, of formation, respect for the dignity of the other, together with the recognition of the values that are ultimately binding for everyone and that have their origin and purpose in God. It is in the light of faith that one can attain

7

that global justice which, together with a world peace, would be able to lead to a universal humanism, in the full sense of the term, pervaded by spiritual values.

In the sphere of the debate concerning the development of man toward a new world, that humanity—which intends to render justice profoundly and forever to the nature of man—is possible only if, starting from faith, it understands itself as a manifestation of that which is at the heart of human coexistence. Pervaded by the commandment of "love your neighbor as yourself," there comes into being a humanity which Christian anthropology formulates in a most clear and efficacious way: to love the other insofar as he is a creature of God, and to love God since he revealed himself to us as the Creator, the Savior, and as the one who brings the humanity of man to fulfillment. From here, one must draw the substance for the response to the question about how our world ought to function; on how it would find God; on what value it would base itself; and the kind of dignity that man would possess.

Highlighting Man as a Created Being, in Service to His Dignity

The encyclicals of Pope Paul VI and St. John Paul II sought to have us question ourselves on the idea of progress with a new approach. Is the vocation of man truly that for which, in the historical process, he proceeds toward a world that is always more perfect, ever more economically mature, and always more advanced on the technical level? Does the ultimate victory over oppression and suffering, over needs and death consist in mechanistic progress? Or instead, together with economic and social transformations, do we tend to affirm a false image of man that sees in him only a consumer or a part of the market, in such a way as to open up new possibilities for the economic factor? This process—which the encyclical *Sollicitudo Rei Socialis* sees as founded on a "naive mechanistic optimism"[5]— did not succeed in changing for the better the situation in vast areas of the planet. Comfort and richness, but also political stability and dignified and just conditions of life, continue to remain the unique prerogative of one part of humanity. However, the material and spiritual goods of the earth must be placed at the disposal of everyone because they are for everyone.

Thus, the results obtained with that process go to the advantage of a restricted group, whose richness grows infinitely, while for the poor and indigent the so greatly proclaimed progress often reveals itself as a way toward an even greater misery and oppression.

For the Church, human development consists essentially in the service of the dignity of man: in progress toward an authentic humanity as it is amply described in the encyclical.[6]

Authentic human development consists in engagement in favor of the dignity of man who, in a society that structures itself in a new way, must become a platform to overturn concretely in practice that which defines the authentic humanity of man.[7]

One must never lose sight of this parameter: the specific nature of man, created by God in his image and likeness (See Gn 1:26). The corporal and spiritual natures are symbolized in the second account of creation from two elements: the earth, with which God formed the physical part of man, and the breath of life, breathed into his nostrils (See Gn 2:7). Authentic human development must therefore find fulfillment in a framework of solidarity and freedom: "The obligation to commit oneself to the development of peoples is not just an individual duty, and still less an individualistic one, as if it were possible to achieve this development through the isolated efforts of each individual. It is an imperative which obliges each and every man and woman, as well as societies and nations. In particular, it obliges the Catholic Church."[8] With these words, St. John Paul II highlights the responsibility that, starting with the individual, must be assumed by the various forms of the human community: states, nations, Europe, the United Nations, the entire world, and every man. All are at the service of men and women, their development, their formation, their sustenance, and their property. Cooperation for the development of the whole man and of all people is a duty of everyone toward everyone and must be equally distributed on the shoulders of the entire planet.

Particular responsibility falls on the countries that live in comfort. However, they must not allow themselves to be led to offer only economic and technical assistance, thus making the countries that live in poverty and in need to understand that they are in the final analysis mere groups of consumers and, with that, an object of the market and of big transnational groups, thus obliging them to assume the lifestyle of pure consumerism.

Human development, from the point of view of our condition as creatures, is *in primis et ante omnia* a moral notion which is and must be in harmony with a type of progress favoring the individual and the authentic nature of man. Therefore, man must be understood in his historical, cultural, political, and psychological reality. Opposition to an unregulated "commercialization" of the poorest countries has its foundation in the recognition of those original cultural and historical structures that mark the peoples of those nations with their seal and form man from the beginning of his existence.

This recognition presupposes the willingness and the capacity to see in the other someone who is similar, who in faith becomes our neighbor, at whose side I stand helping him and reinforcing him in that which is proper to him, and not instead taking from him his autonomy and right to self-determination.

"Let us make human beings in our image, after our likeness." (Gn 1:26)

Authentic human development stands at the foundation of moral norms, which, as created beings, we can take from the commandments of God. From these commandments emerges a profound and complex knowledge of human life, of the decisions flowing from it, and of the weaknesses that are co-natural to it. The First Commandment is the basis for a life starting with the certainty that God is not far from us: rather that he accompanies us along our path, guiding our lives into his truth and love.

Daily the mass media tell us about conflicts, divisions, wars, atrocities, and terror; and every day the sadness and dispersion of a world without God becomes clearer. God, in fact, has called us to a communion that is much more profound than the political-institutional systems, or than mundane forms of association.

We, in fact, belong to the Church of Jesus Christ, which is his Body, and of which he himself is the Head. This dimension of man has disappeared in vast areas of the earth. It is necessary to underscore continuously the dimension of the sacramentality of the Church, a sign placed in the world and for the world, capable of orienting the world to God and rendering him present in time. We are members of the Church and thus, in the experience of transcendence, overcome all the barriers that man has constructed.

When we speak of the development of man, we must say that his relationship with the transcendent is part of it. In being a creature of God, man therefore finds fulfillment in God. One who makes man believe that his life takes place only within the limits of time and between the dates that circumscribe his life, in reality robs his life of the dimension of hope, forgiveness, love, and redemption.

At the same time, he escapes from the one who helps and protects the reason for his action, since he will see in that person only "the other" or even only an enemy. But in God, the Creator, the being of man made in the image of God becomes the sign of his dignity: "The Christian who is taught to see that man is the image of God, called to share in the truth and the good which is God himself, does not understand a commitment to development and its application which excludes regard and respect for the unique dignity of this 'image.'"[9] In other words, true development must be founded on the love of God and neighbor and must contribute to the fostering of relations between individuals and societies. Hence, the "civilization of love," of which Pope Paul VI often spoke.

Called to Love

St. John Paul II, in his encyclical *Centesimus Annus*, presented a type of "charter," almost an appeal, in which he described the fundamental Christian conception of the nature of man: "Among the most important of these rights, mention must be made of the right to life, an integral part of which is the right of the child to develop in the mother's womb from the moment of conception; the right to live in a united family and in a moral environment conducive to the growth of the child's personality; the right to develop one's intelligence and freedom in seeking and knowing the truth; the right to share in the work which makes wise use of the earth's material resources, and to derive from that work the means to support oneself and one's dependents; and the right freely to establish a family, to have and to rear children."[10]

With his focus turned toward the Apostolic Exhortation *Familiaris Consortio* of 1981, St. John Paul II continues his reflection, thus developing the anthropology that defines his entire pontificate: God has called man to love. Thus, at the center of Christian anthropology is the family. The family must be protected as a place in which every person, lovingly received, matures, becoming the one who, in giving of himself, in willingness to sacrifice, becomes an integrated person. Thus does he develop and, by way of reflection, he finds his true self and realizes himself. The family is the natural place of man's becoming, of human flourishing. Christian anthropology does not lose itself in vague conjectures but has secure points of reference and is based on very concrete convictions. We often become aware of their presence and strength only when they are put aside or denied.

For this reason, when we speak of the authentic development of man, we must consider that the family is the germinal cell of faith, the refuge for an authentic growth, and the space of a loving solidarity; it is also the first great stadium of true human "progress."

Creature and Person: Cornerstones of Human Rights

Already St. John XXIII, in the encyclical *Pacem in Terris*, presented his own "Magna Charta" of human rights. With this encyclical, he surpasses the Universal Declaration of Human Rights, thanks to that clear Christian connotation that pervades the question in *Pacem in Terris*. In fact, the point of departure of the dignity of man is seen in his personal being. In this way, the Church surpasses the horizontal motivations—which can be easily modified on their own—instead orienting the debate to its authentic nucleus: gifted with reason and free will, the person, his personality, has rights and duties of his own by his very nature. His respect must be recognized by all as a shared base of action. Only thus is born a true possibility of eliminating the injustice and the blinding inequalities regarding the access to and distribution of the goods of the earth, the possibilities to make use of freedom, valid for every man, the focal point of all social ordinances: "Any well-regulated and productive association of men in society demands the acceptance of one fundamental principle: that each individual man is truly a person. His is a nature, that is, endowed with intelligence and free will. As such he has rights and duties, which together flow as a direct consequence from his nature. These rights and duties are universal and inviolable, and therefore altogether inalienable."[11]

The basic idea of human rights not only corresponds intimately to the Judeo-Christian concept of man, but is also the root from which all the initiatives geared to the valuing of human life spread. By means of the Church, such foundations become, so to speak, translated into the modern world. Ethnic, political differences or those of a cultural identity must never become a barrier among men. Every form of marginalization contrasts with the idea of the person clearly defined by the Church.

Overcoming religious, national, and ideological barriers, the Church can actively contribute to the definition of a pre-juridic consensus with respect to the dignity and rights of man. Christian responsibility concerning human rights becomes evident in the formation of a public awareness and also in action with respect to all the questions that touch the inviolability of the human being. The Church takes a position on legislation geared to the defense of human life and acts by means of charitable organizations at the international level (which contribution does not limit itself to immediate measures of help and of support for long-term projects, going well beyond only material help). The task of the Church in the field of poverty, where conditions of minimal sustenance are lacking, helps the one who suffers to rediscover his proper human dignity, or even to become aware of it for the first time.

Evangelium Vitae and Deus Caritas Est

In the first encyclical of Pope Benedict XVI, *Deus Caritas Est*, he stressed: "The Church's charitable organizations, on the other hand, constitute an *opus proprium*, a task agreeable to her, in which she does not cooperate collaterally, but acts as a subject with direct responsibility, doing what corresponds to her nature. The Church can never be exempted from practicing charity as an organized activity of believers, and on the other hand, there will never be a situation where the charity of each individual Christian is unnecessary, because in addition to justice man needs, and will always need, love."[12]

If we take up again what was said before, then it appears truly evident that man would find his most authentic vocation in love toward God and toward those like him.

It is then that freedom in solidarity reaches its proper realization; equality—among individuals and among peoples—overflows into an enduring peace, the defense of life for all the stages of the development of the human-individual, and the justice that is based on the search for truth. Only then does the dignity of man become the criterion for relationships and at the same time the first and indisputable way of access to the nature of man.

The task of the Church is to counterpose this "Gospel of life"—to cite the title that St. John Paul II wanted to give to one of his encyclicals[13]—to the culture of death and to overcome threats and dangers with the proclamation of the good news, underscoring the incomparable value of the human person, his greatness and preciousness: "The Gospel of God's love for man, the Gospel of the dignity of the person and the Gospel of life are a single and indivisible Gospel."[14]

"Every individual,"—and with this quotation I conclude—"precisely by reason of the mystery of the Word of God who was made flesh (cf. Jn 1:14), is entrusted to the maternal care of the Church. Therefore, every threat to human dignity and life must necessarily be felt in the Church's very heart; it cannot but affect her at the core of her faith in the Redemptive Incarnation of the Son of God, and engage her in her mission of proclaiming the Gospel of life in all the world and to every creature (cf. Mk 16:15)."[15]

III. Liberation Theology Today

With the dramatic crisis of the hostages in the residence of the Japanese ambassador in Lima that went on for weeks, the explosive situation of Peru and of all of Latin America jumped powerfully to the attention of global public opinion.[16] Revolutionary movements, civil wars, and terrorism are not the causes, but are the unambiguous symptoms of the devastating socioeconomic condition in which the majority of the persons of that continent are embroiled.

After the fall of the Berlin Wall and the Communist bloc, to many observers it seemed only a question of time before Latin America would abandon the resistance and the protest, to which liberation theology gave a voice, against the exploitation and centuries-long oppression carried out first by the colonial powers and then afterward by centers of economic power in North America and Europe.

The "natural" division of roles between rich and poor countries seemed to be in the balance again. Only the virus of Marxism—as it was said—can be responsible for the fact that, suddenly, people rebelled against their abuse as being underpaid labor forces and against the removal, at ridiculous prices, of the prime materials of their homeland. It would be seen as only the fault of this virus if these people no longer desired to forego basic health care, a state-run administration founded on law and justice, an academic formation, and dignified housing. The triumphalism of a capitalism that presumed itself to be victorious went hand and hand with the satisfaction for which liberation theology's own foundation seemed to fall short. It was thought to be easy to associate liberation theology with revolutionary violence and the terrorism of Marxist groups. In the notorious secret document prepared for President Ronald Reagan in 1980, the Committee of Santa Fe solicited the government of the United States of America to proceed in a military manner against "liberation theology" and the Catholic Church in Latin America that bore its imprint: "The role of the Church in Latin America is of vital importance for the concept of political liberty. Unfortunately, the Marxist-Leninist forces have used the Church as a political arm against private property and the system of capitalist production, insofar as ideas which are more Communist than Christian have infiltrated the religious community."[17]

What is more disconcerting in that document is the shamelessness with which its drafters, responsible for brutal military dictatorships and powerful oligarchies, exalted their interest for private property and for the capitalist system of production as a criterion for determining what is or is not Christian. It must be clear to the European reader that private property in Latin America is not that little portion of goods that one procures with a lifetime of sacrifices and privations; rather, private property is concerned with enormous estates or, for example, entire mines of copper and silver, in the face of millions of little farmers or peasants deprived of every possession and right. This is also the background against which to understand the economic and political support given to the fundamentalist sects and to their activity. With these, there is a desire to reject the fight of liberation theology in favor of an integral vision, embracing grace and redemption, while also reducing the role of religion to a mere other-worldly consolation, all enclosed within the private sphere; and so one uses religion as a stabilizing factor for an unjust society. A particularly grave example of the damage caused to human rights is given from the fact that certain institutions of North America make the furnishing of foods and provisions to Peru dependent on the commitment to adopt politics that are geared to a drastic lowering of the birth rate. This condition was seconded by the Peruvian government, so that on the pretext of having to submit men and women to certain tests, unbeknownst to them and against their will, contraceptive means rendering them definitively sterile were imposed.

In this case, the key word seems to be this: struggle against poverty by means of the decimation of the poor. One supposes that poverty is caused by a high birth rate, thus drawing attention away

16

from poverty's true causes. In Peru, which is five times bigger than Germany and which has a percentage of inhabitants five times less than that of Germany, one cannot quite speak of overpopulation. One who sees with his own eyes the countless forms of degradation leveled against individuals—forms of enslavement and abuse—cannot allow himself to be deceived by such a hymn of praise to efficiency and the superiority of capitalism. Nevertheless, to avoid equivocations, it is necessary to make a clarification with respect to the term "capitalism."

In the Latin American context, the word "capitalism" mirrors a style of life that, raised up to the ultimate criterion of human achievement, tends toward untethered personal enrichment. This type of capitalism has nothing to do with a free economy of enterprise, of market, in which persons invest their own work and their own capacities, cooperating in the building up and functioning of a social economy, in the context of a state of democratically constituted law.

In the face of the failure of this capitalist system in its worst form and of the corresponding mentality that disparages human rights, liberation theology retains a burning relevance. The element that fundamentally distinguishes liberation theology from a Marxist system and from a capitalist system is precisely that element which profoundly unites those two systems, although with all the contrary positions that define their relationship: it is, therefore, that conception of man and of society common to both according to which God, Jesus Christ, and the Gospel cannot have any role for the humanization of man, neither as an individual aspect, nor as a member of society.

And yet liberation theology will not die as long as there are people who allow themselves to be affected by the liberating action of God and who create solidarity for the suffering, whose dignity is trampled: the measure of their faith and the incentive for their action in society. Liberation theology means, in brief, to believe in God as the God of life and as the guarantor of a salvation understood in its fullness, resisting the gods and idols responsible for premature deaths, poverty, and the degradation of man.

Gustavo Gutierrez: The Man, the Christian, and the Theologian

The term "liberation theology" goes back to a conference held by Gustavo Gutierrez in 1968 in Cimbote, in the north of Peru. The term then provided the title for his book *Teología de la Liberación* (1971); with this book, liberation theology acquired notoriety in the entire world. The tenth edition of the book (1992) also has an ample introduction. There the author clarifies the significance of some terms, susceptible to misunderstandings: for example, that of preferential option for the poor, class struggle, the theory of dependence, and structural and social sin. Here Gutierrez also deconstructs in a convincing way the accusations brought against it of horizontalism and of making Christianity too focused on the immanent.

Gutierrez, considered by many to be the father of liberation theology, makes evident that it is not a theoretical construction invented at a desk. Liberation theology sees itself in continuity with the complex development of Catholic theology in the twentieth and twenty-first centuries. In this sense, faced with new sociological structures, liberation theology emerged from the transition to the modern industrial society, to the globalization of markets, and to the linking together of information systems, and made reference to the social teachings of the popes, starting with the Encyclical *Rerum Novarum* of Pope Leo XIII, then *Populorum Progressio* of Pope Paul VI, and also of St. John XXIII, who affirmed how the Church must stand on the side of the poor. To this are joined the great texts of the Magisterium of St. John Paul II and his actions.

A very significant font for liberation theology is the Pastoral Constitution of Vatican II, *Gaudium et Spes*, on the Church in the modern world. Already in *Lumen Gentium*, the Council had presented the Church not as a religious community separated from the world and self-sufficient, but as the sacrament of salvation for the world. The Church, working as a sign and instrument of the union of God with men and of men among themselves, is the handmaiden of salvation that God constituted in history, once for all and definitively in Jesus Christ: that salvation which, by means of the Holy

Spirit, he has established as the perennial principle of human history and of the building up of a society worthy of man.

And so, the great conferences of the Latin American episcopate of Medellín (1968), Puebla (1979), and Santo Domingo (1992) understood themselves as putting into practice and realizing the entire development of Catholic theology of the twentieth century, in the sociocultural and spiritual context of the Latin American subcontinent. For this reason, a new understanding of the Church comes about, starting with Vatican II, which spread to all of Latin America. That conciliar conception of the Church is completely incompatible with the division—going back to the colonial period, whose effects make themselves felt even today—between a restricted group of leaders, bishops, priests, and religious belonging to the white population: or, respectively, to missionaries from foreign countries on the one hand and, on the other hand, to a group composed of the descendants of slaves of color and of mixed race who are considered immature and to whom are offered only religious rites.

Today, lay people on the whole—men and women, as well as an ever-growing number of indigenous priests, of catechists, and of religious women—are aware of being bearers of the entire mission of the Church. The countless grassroots communities are a living proof of the immediate identification of the people with the Church. The Church is no longer only the Church for the people or the Church of the people. The Church is the People of God among the peoples of the world and coming from the peoples of the earth; the Church is thus the People of God for the world. The poor and the marginalized, through a profound and intimate encounter with the Gospel, understand themselves in their dignity as persons in the presence of God, participating actively in the life of the ecclesial community and thus fulfilling the mission of the Church as the sacrament of salvation for the world. From it is derived a new concept of theology. The professional theologian is not placed above the faithful or the profane as an expert in religious matters. Rather, he begins to share their sufferings and hopes. In this sense, liberation theology is a theology matured in the community; it is a contextualized theology in the best sense of the term. Thus also overcome is the gap between an erudite academic theology and the reflection of the believer on the concrete experiences of the communities.

Among the best known works of Gutierrez are *La Fuerza histórica de los pobres* (1979) and *Beber en su proprio pozo* (1981). In the latter work, whose title is taken from a noted expression of St. Bernard of Clairvaux, Gutierrez intends to demonstrate the spiritual foundation of liberation theology. In *Dios o el oro en las Indias* (1989), he shows the liberating way undertaken by Bartolomé de las Casas, the famous Dominican who became a bishop and who, at the beginning of Spanish colonization, along with other Dominican and Jesuit theologians, was a pioneer in the struggle for the human rights of the *Indios* and for the defense of their dignity.

Still unknown is the fact that there were, most of all, Spanish theologians (among them Francisco de Victoria) who with their critique set up a safeguard for the aboriginal Latin American population, already two centuries before the Enlightenment, and who placed on the agenda the themes of human rights and the rights of the peoples. *Las Casas* is also the title of a monumental biography of the noted Dominican, which appeared in 1992.

It is possible to affirm with certitude that A *Theology of Liberation* has acquired a considerable place among the classics of theology of the second half of the twentieth century.

Gutierrez has often wanted to clear the field of misunderstanding—that sympathizers and adversaries of liberation theology have in common—that liberation theology would be limited to the work of theologians interested above all in the social and political dimension of human life, spreading itself out into spheres extraneous to them: the spheres of the economy, politics, and sociology, losing in this way the authentic object of theology, the fundamental relationship of man with God. However, if one studies liberation theology's starting point seriously, one will not be very surprised about its foundation, which is strictly theocentric and christocentric, as well as its being anchored in the living community of the Church.

In the context of secularization in Europe, Dietrich Bonhoeffer had envisioned in the nonbeliever the authentic interlocutor of Christian theology, asking the question: "How is it possible to speak of God in a world that has become emancipated?" Similarly, Gustavo Gutierrez, addressing the Latin American population whose majority is Christian asks: "How can one speak of God when one sees so much suffering, premature death, and the continually violated dignity of the poor of Latin America?"

Gutierrez had received from his teachers of theology—like Maurice Blondel, Henri de Lubac, Juan Alfaro, and Karl Rahner—that interior impulse to link together in a profound way speaking of God with a concrete taking of a position for the man who awaits from God a holistic salvation. Having studied medicine and literature, Gutierrez turned to philosophy and psychology, a course of studies that he concluded with a thesis on Sigmund Freud. He decided to undertake studies in theology relatively late, after having received the priestly vocation. He was ordained in Lima at thirty-one years of age. It is clear that the minimal common denominator of a course of studies so varied is love for man, the desire to care for him. His teachers formed him with respect to the debate, current in that time, concerning the relationship between nature and grace and which is decisive in determining the whole relationship between Christianity and that image of secularized and autonomous man, fruit of the European Enlightenment and of modernity. The question can be summed up thus: Do two parallel orders exist, that is to say, a secular autonomous end of man and a supernatural revelation, such that man would move in two spheres of knowledge and life, completely separate and independent of one another? Or instead, is man called by God in his most profound unity as a person and, in that which represents his heart, to build up religiously and ethically a personal and social life?

A theological conceptual scheme of thought that considers revelation as a synthesis of the liberation of man brought about by God and as the cooperation of man with the work of God that frees and redeems—a scheme of thought like this—sees an inseparable correlation between creation and redemption, between faith and living in the world, between transcendence and immanence, between history and eschatology, between an exclusively spiritual relationship with Christ and the upsetting of it in a life lived in external discipleship. Thus liberation theology overcomes the rigid schematization of a dualism that counterposes the life hereafter to life here-and-now, and in which religion is reduced to a mystical experience of the individual and an individualistic morality: a functional morality to obtain as a reward a better life in the afterlife.

Liberation theology does not mean a new revelation. Rather, it seeks to be a new way of presenting the cooperation of Christians in the transformation of the world on God's part. Therefore, Gutierrez arrives directly at a presentation of it in these terms: "The theology of liberation offers us not so much a new theme for reflection as a *new way* to do theology. Theology as critical reflection on historical praxis is a liberating theology, a theology of the liberating transformation of the history of mankind and also therefore that part of mankind—gathered into *ecclesia*—which openly confesses Christ. This is a theology which does not stop with reflecting on the world, but rather tries to be part of the process through which the world is transformed. It is a theology which is open—in protest against a trampled human dignity, in the struggle against the plunder of the vast majority of people, in liberating love, and in the building of a new, just, and fraternal society—to the gift of the Kingdom of God."[18]

It is important to stress that redemption and liberation are synonymous with the holistic, integral relationship of man with God who, in Jesus Christ, has bent toward suffering man in need of salvation. Gutierrez distinguishes three levels of liberation: firstly, from sin, taken as the most profound rupture of friendship with God and with other men and, therefore, the root of every form of the enslavement of man, whether in an interior or exterior sense. Secondly, this expresses itself as the necessity of liberation from interior slavery of an untethered thirst for profit. This comes about, thirdly, in the attempt to overcome, as a disciple of Christ, the oppression, marginalization, abuse, and socioeconomic misdeeds that flow from it and which constitute social and structural sin as a manifestation of personal sin.

In this context, it is necessary to make some precisions concerning the concepts of *poverty* and *hunger*. From a biblical perspective, poverty signifies above all else the degrading misery of man, and then the connotation of the total need for salvation of men, to whom the Gospel is proclaimed. Finally, poverty is spiritual openness and availability for service of the Kingdom of God. The invitation to poverty in the evangelical sense does not at all signify that a Christian voluntarily would choose to live in a condition that degrades human dignity. The religious who makes a vow of poverty renounces personal property in order to participate thus fully in the mission of the religious community, to put himself entirely at the service of the sick and the poor, or also at the service of educational and formative activity in the school and university. It is in this sense that the already-famous expression of St. John Paul II is also to be understood who, in a letter to the Brazilian Episcopal Conference in 1986, underscored how liberation theology was "not only opportune, but useful and necessary." It was evidently precisely this thought that inspired him when, a year earlier, at Villa El Salvador, a poor neighborhood of Lima, before millions of people, he exclaimed: "The hunger for bread must be conquered; the hunger for God must remain."

Liberation Theology as Standard-Bearer of the Mission of the Church

Liberation theology, as developed by Gutierrez, is not a sociology dressed up as theology. Liberation theology is theology in the strict sense. It does not preach class struggle, but how to overcome the antagonism that exists among classes and groups of power and also of racism, elements from which flow poverty and the despisal of the dignity of the greater part of humanity.

The foundation of liberation theology is the faith that God has created man in his image and that, in his Son, Jesus Christ, he cares for man, even to the point of Jesus accepting the death to which his adversaries had condemned him. The objective of this is to make God recognizable as the God of life and as the conqueror of death in all the dimensions of human existence. Liberation theology overcomes every dualism that would relegate God to the hereafter and reduce salvation to a mere interior dimension.

Man stands in the profound tension of "being called" by God in creation, in the history of salvation, and in the expectation of its fulfillment, beyond the limits of the individual's death and the complex purpose of history. Christian faith means participating intelligently and actively in the process of the transformation of history that God, in the salvific activity of Jesus Christ, has definitively inaugurated as a path toward him.

In this way, a three-fold methodology follows as a consequence.

First: In the faith and following of Jesus, Christians actively participate in the liberating activity of God for the personal dignity of man and for his salvation. In analyzing society, liberation theology also draws from the methods of the human and social sciences. In this we find the distinction of liberation theology from classical theology, in that it does not dialogue only with philosophy. Precisely on this point are justified the critical points made by the Congregation for the Doctrine of the Faith (*Libertatis Nuntius*, 1984): this intends to highlight the necessity of distinguishing between the results of the social sciences from the ideological deviations coming from them. As is known, the second *Instruction* of the Congregation for the Doctrine of the Faith (*Libertatis Conscientia*, 1986) accords value *latu sensu* to a theology of liberty correctly understood.

A second methodological step results: a social analysis, or a critical and rational reflection in the light of the Gospel and of revelation on the national and international causes of mass poverty, as well as on its historical and structural dimensions.

A third step, finally, is geared toward an active transformation, critically thought out, of empirical reality: because the objective is the dominion of God on the earth as thus announced by Jesus. The dominion of God is to be understood here as a dynamic principle that, in the concreteness of the condition of people who suffer the effects of estrangement from God, becomes the transforming principle in human, social, and individual life on earth. Hence is derived the preferential option for the poor and for people deprived of their human dignity. The option for the poor does not exclude the rich because they are also meant to receive the liberating work of God, freed from the anguish for which they think they must realize their own life by taking away the life of others. Whether in regard to the poor or the rich, the liberating action of God tends to their transformation into authentic human subjects, hence, free from any form of oppression and dependence.

Already in the Old Testament, in the experience of the Exodus, is demonstrated how redemption is understood as liberating work. God does not consign the enslaved Israelites to a better afterlife, but instead leads them into the Promised Land, which is a land of freedom. The liberating work of God culminates in the event of Christ. Jesus announces the Kingdom of God as Gospel for the poor, the excluded, the sick. Moreover, Jesus showed forth the liberating work of God when confronted with the resistance of sinners, in giving proof, even unto his own death, of the love of God as the foundation of human existence, in life and in death. Through the Cross and death of Jesus, God has elevated the world to the rank of reality in which a new creation is revealed. For this reason, the Cross is the revelation of the option of God for the suffering, the disenfranchised, the tortured, the murdered. In the Resurrection of Jesus from the dead, God has shown in an original and exemplary way what life is precisely; he has demonstrated how freedom can be realized in being for others and in a struggle for obtaining conditions of life that are worthy of man.

One can characterize better the significance and importance of Gustavo Gutierrez as a theologian and also as a convinced Christian with the words that conclude his most famous work:

> The theology of liberation attempts to reflect on the experience and meaning of the faith based on the commitment to abolish injustice and to build a new society. . . . If theological reflection does not vitalize the action of the Christian community in the world by making its commitment to charity fuller and more radical, if—more concretely—in Latin America it does not lead the Church to be on the side of the oppressed classes

and dominated peoples, clearly and without qualifications, then this theological reflection will have been of little value. . . . We must be careful not to fall into an intellectual self-satisfaction, into a kind of triumphalism of erudite and advanced "new" visions of Christianity. The only thing that is really new is to accept day by day the gift of the Spirit, who makes us love—in our concrete options to build a true human brotherhood, in our historical initiatives to subvert an order of injustice—with the fullness with which Christ loved us. To paraphrase a well-known text of Pascal, we can say that all the political theologies, the theologies of hope, of revolution, and of liberation, are not worth one act of genuine solidarity with exploited classes. They are not worth one act of faith, love, and, hope, committed—in one way or another—in active participation to liberate man from everything that dehumanizes him and prevents him from living according to the will of the Father.[19]

IV. "Test everything; retain what is good." (1 Thes 5:21): Twenty-Five Years After the Instruction *Libertatis Conscientia* on Liberation Theology

In the tenth volume of the *Gesammelte Schriften* of Joseph Ratzinger, which came out in February 2012 and which takes eschatology as its point of departure, texts on liberation theology were inserted. Twenty-five years ago, the Instruction of the Congregation for the Doctrine of the Faith on Christian freedom and liberation, entitled *Libertatis Conscientia*, was published and signed by the then-Prefect, Cardinal Joseph Ratzinger. It contains the magisterial evaluation of liberation theology developed in Latin America. It is worth reading because the surprising foresight of that document emerges. The personal affirmations of Joseph Ratzinger on liberation theology examine in great depth the tendency, perceived in it, to politicize theology and to reduce the Church to a series of this-worldly activities. For this reason, Ratzinger saw the very nature of the Church and of theology as being a topic for discussion. Here one is not dealing with expressing an impulse or unmotivated "yes" or "no" concerning liberation theology; rather, it seeks to bring about a *profound clarification* with regard to its positive aspects, as well as to its limitations and dangers. Liberation theology embraces a number of concepts and authors that differ among themselves to some degree. Nevertheless, at the base of liberation theology there is a fundamental question: when faced with conditions of life that damage human dignity, how can the message of God's love, the transforming power of the Gospel, become effective in the life of individuals and of the community?

"Catholic" Liberation Theology?

Every concept of liberation theology remains Catholic so long as its entire hermeneutic is that of the real, salvific revelation of God himself in his Son, Jesus Christ, whose faithful interpretation has been entrusted to the Church through the *sensus fidei* of all the faithful and of the Magisterium of the bishops and the pope. Both documents of the Congregation for the Doctrine of the Faith of 1984 and of 1986 (*Libertatis Nuntius* and *Libertatis Conscientia*) resolve to keep the "theologies of liberation" from becoming ideologies, thus preserving their character as theology. The second Instruction of 1986 intends to bring about profound differentiations in this sense. It condemns those tendencies that lose sight of the supernatural and follow concepts of processes of liberation and of apparently enlightened revolutions but which, in reality, are mythological. Similar theologies were considered definitive only as a super-structure of a Marxist project. *Libertatis Conscientia* shows, on the other hand, the authentic Christian concept of man and the world, and thus makes level the road to a true liberation theology that is closely joined to the social doctrine of the Church and that can and must make its proper voice heard precisely in today's world. It is a concept that, starting from a faith perspective, is aware of the entire historical reality of man—whether as an individual or in society—and offers directives for action not only to the individual Christian but also with respect to the great political and economic choices.

The affirmations regarding Christology and soteriology, the doctrine of grace and anthropology cannot be reinterpreted in a merely existentialist and revolutionary political manner, thus degenerating into elements of a social program of self-redemption. The faith cannot be reduced to the affirmation for which it would be nothing other than "fidelity to history," "hope in looking to the future," and similar things. In reality, faith, hope, and love are theological virtues, gifts of grace that, however, must necessarily have as a consequence responsibility for the world and for history: the option for the poor. Love of God and love of one's neighbor are inseparably joined. But love for God above all things is an authentic reality and is not addressed to a fictitious person in the afterlife, insofar as it is an appeal to a responsible social action. In the teaching of the Fathers and of the Scholastics on the different "senses" of Scripture, the moral sense presupposes the historical sense and postulates it, and does not vanish in it.

The Gospel: Proclamation of Freedom and Liberation

The point of departure of *Libertatis Conscientia* is the "awareness of man's freedom and dignity," which moves all the people of the whole world and which "is one of the major characteristics of our time."[20] Since the Gospel "is by its very nature a message of freedom and liberation,"[21] the Church can make those aspirations her own.

The abandonment of the concept of liberty whose basic criterion is anarchy and whose way is the systematic elimination of every bond; the distinction between the supernatural order of salvation and the temporal order of human life that must be seen from within the unique design of God, which is to recapitulate all things in Christ; all of this, affirms the document, confers on Christian liberty as a grace a continual dynamism whose purpose is to actualize earthly conditions of life that are marked by human dignity, freedom, justice, peaceful coexistence in the sphere of the family, the state, and the global community.

"Liberation" Without Violence

A glance at the Scriptures reveals that the history of the covenant is the history of liberation, with an option of God, that emerges always more clearly for the poor, the needy, and those who are abused, in such a way that soteriology also demands ethics. "The liberating mission of the Church" says the fundamental fourth chapter of the Instruction, has its origins in the message of freedom and liberation of Jesus and in the very action of Jesus. The Church affirms in a positive manner "the foundations of justice in the temporal order"[22] and "thus the Church is being faithful to her mission when she condemns the forms of deviation, slavery and oppression of which people are victims."[23] However, in conformity with her mission, the Church condemns all methods with which one responds to violence with violence, to terror with terror, to the suppression of rights with the suppression of rights.

The Contribution of Christians for a Just Society

In spiritual and material evils that afflict a great part of humanity through unjust systems, the Church fulfills "the preferential option for the poor,"[24] not to cause conflicts to break out, but for the purpose of breaking down barriers among classes and of creating solidarity, human dignity, and subsidiarity as the foundations of social order. With respect to the relationship between personal sin and structures, one must say that there exists "a structure of sin"[25] as a result of erroneous collective developments and as an expression of mistaken mentalities. These structures can be called sinful because they are the fruit of sin and lead to sin. But this does not exclude individual responsibility. No one can be justified in saying that he has been coerced by the system to take advantage of other human beings and to send them into ruin so that he could guarantee a life for himself.

The Liberating Practice of Christians:
The Civilization of Love

The so-called historically necessary processes do not determine man in a fatalistic fashion, taking from him the free use of his responsibility before God. Neither "destiny" nor the "laws of history," but the *Providentia Dei* determines the course of history with respect to human liberty and its fulfillment in love, whether that concerns this life or the order of the supernatural vocation of man.

The priority of the person over structure remains. For this reason, the liberating practice of Christians—which derives from the liberation from sin and from the communication of grace—has as a consequence both the change and continual betterment of the material and social conditions of life and the personal encounter between human beings in the love of Christ.

> Christians working to bring about that "civilization of love" which will include the entire ethical and social heritage of the Gospel are today faced with an unprecedented challenge. This task calls for renewed reflection on what constitutes the relationship between the supreme commandment of love and the social order considered in all its complexity. The immediate aim of this in-depth reflection is to work out and set in motion ambitious programs aimed at the socio-economic liberation of millions of men and women caught in an intolerable situation of economic, social and political oppression. This action must begin with an immense effort at education: education for the civilization of work, education for solidarity, access to culture for all.[26]

Such an effort is necessary for the Church, and is helpful for the poor and indigent of the whole world.

This Instruction of the Congregation for the Doctrine of the Faith has therefore helped to identify the positive content of new theological approaches and has shown how "an authentic liberation theology" (St. John Paul II) and the social doctrine of the Catholic Church are essential for the service of the Church in the world. All must seek to make operative the Christian doctrine of liberty and the dignity of man.

The Evangelizing Mission of the Church

I. Faith, The true richness of the Church

Only a Great Positivity Can Attract Our Attention

For a stranger who opens the first page of *The Betrothed* for the first time, the words of Alessandro Manzoni that describe those places of Lake Como—words that for you Italians are perhaps so known and taken for granted—represent an authentic invitation to our reason, almost a contagion.

Opening to the reader, in so rapid but effective a way, that panorama of gulfs, promontories, torrents, valleys, country sides, and views of mountains, Manzoni brings our attention to what is marvelous. The genius of this Milanese writer of the nineteenth century, with few and incisive words, succeeds in making transparent that positivity which nature can disclose to our eyes only on certain days.

Only a great positivity can attract our attention, the horizons of our reason, as Pope Benedict XVI would say, broadening our cognitive capabilities. In fact, before certain spectacles of nature and before certain events, we feel ourselves struck and deeply touched: our whole person and all our freedom feels transported in those spectacles and summoned by them.

It is this transport that draws us into the heart of reality, which we have before our eyes, and this is all the more so on those occasions when we feel at one with what we know. A similar experience also occurs in love. In fact, the first form of love, that of attachment, of which our reason is capable, experiences and documents itself precisely in relationship to reality, encountering such positive passages of reality.

Putting aside my personal admiration for the talent of Alessandro Manzoni, I wanted to begin by making a reference to such experiences because what takes place in man by means of that phenomenon that one calls "faith," at least in its Christian and Catholic connotation, has many analogies to much of what I described above.

Nothing like beauty, goodness, truth, love, seen in reality, are capable of grasping our reason and of launching it onto a cognitive adventure, involving our whole person, including our affectivity, and of giving us fundamental certitudes for existence. Already this fact must then cause us a little doubt about the epistemological objective now taken for granted for several centuries attributed to that critical distance which modern science claims as a condition and guarantee of solid certitudes.

Certainly, there is no one who does not see how the passions and emotions can play bad jokes, diminishing in some cases the sense of reality in one who allows himself to be ruled and dominated by them. Nevertheless, emotion plays a very important role at the cognitive level, and thus we cannot get rid of it without easily causing negative consequences for reason.

Therefore, it is true that without a feeling of authentic interest toward what we know, we cannot truly attain to reality. Those who are involved in scientific and intellectual work are readily aware of this. But someone can realize this easily: for example, even a sick person who has before him a physician who is not truly interested in him.

On the other hand, reality itself, whether in its entirety or in its particulars, is capable of challenging at the same time both reason and human affectivity. In fact, it is precisely thanks to a repeated reaction or *affectus*, that intelligence always knows more of that which is attentively seen.

Only this dynamic is capable of educating human reason for a fundamental humility before things and persons, thanks to a continuous and not presumptuous drawing near to the object of knowledge. Only following this dynamic, inherent in our nature, can we speak of a true journey toward a knowledge that is not content with schemas and models—useful but always limited—but which wants to reach authentic certainties about reality.

This is always true, even if it becomes especially evident only on certain occasions of life. Manzoni has shown it to us forever with the first page of his famous novel. It is enough to let ourselves get involved in the cognitive adventure and to recognize it. It is enough to have loyalty and honesty in following it when it takes us by the hand and, by means of that lake and those mountains, makes us see well beyond.

I do not fear to make bold these considerations and to use these arguments because nothing like what we have said above brings us onto the terrain of "faith." Faith, in fact, is a phenomenon that is born in the man who finds himself in the world and who lives, and knows, and loves, and seeks, and loses, and finds. . . . Faith, therefore, springs up and flowers as an event that involves both reason and affectivity, within that adventurous challenge that is reality.

The World as Epiphany of God

The very reality of the world, in its totality and by means of particularly significant experiences, offers to the intelligence and will of man a place of revelation of meanings, from the littlest to the greatest, and from the challenge to search for that which more strongly attracts him.

God himself created the reality of the world as a place of epiphany, of suggestion, and of research, so that people who "grope for him" (Acts 17:27) would seek him and would even find him. God himself has presented things to the eyes of man, so that knowing them, from the simple things—transcending them—he would arrive at the more profound things, scaling the steps of reality to the mystery, the root from which everything proceeds and which underlies all things.

Hence, why the most acute minds of humanity have always perceived certain knowledge as the soil and beginning of totally other knowledge: for example, the knowledge of that which is good, beautiful, and true, as the suggestion of that which is still greater, in a motion of reason without end toward the ultimate goal.

Therefore, Augustine of Hippo, Father and Doctor of the Church, senses the mystery of God thus positively inscribed in human existence and experience and feels it vibrate in the most significant events of life:

> God, the Father of truth, the Father of wisdom, the Father of the true and crowning life, the Father of blessedness, the Father of that which is good and fair, the Father of intelligible light, the Father of our awakening and illumination, the Father of the pledge by which we are admonished to return to Thee.
>
> Thee I invoke, O God, the Truth, in whom and from whom and through whom all things are true which anywhere are true. God, the Wisdom, in whom and from whom and through whom all things are wise which anywhere are wise. God, the true and crowning Life, in whom and from whom and through whom all things live, which truly and supremely live. God, the Blessedness, in whom and from whom and through whom all things are blessed, which anywhere are blessed.[27]

This movement of reason, from the fragments of reality which it knows toward a sense that engrafts them but at the same time transcends them, this passage from the surface of things to their depth, even to the root that constitutes them and from which they flow, is inscribed in the very knowledge of the act of faith. Faith, in fact, recognizes the reality of the world as a sign, as a phenomenon that returns us to the depth in which it is anchored, in some way, and on which it depends *in radice*.

For the rest, whenever we recognize an objective meaning, we pass from the dispersion and from the surface of the elements to the intrinsic connection among them and, therefore, in a certain sense, we begin to reach their deeper reality and their foundation or the *noumenous*. Therefore, unsustainable in an absolute way is the Kantian reduction of the movement from the phenomenon to the foundation.

The hiatus between the phenomenon and the foundation of reality, as the inaccessibility of the *noumenous*, is truly capable of being affirmed only relatively, since already at the cognitive level of our reason, through the world of meanings, it finds itself projected onto an itinerary which moves it toward the foundation of reality, passing from the lesser meanings to those that are greater and ultimate. An epistemological loyalty allows us to recognize that reason can travel along a good stretch of this path, even if its forces are not capable of reaching the final and conclusive levels.

Intellectus Quaerens Fidem, Fides Quaerens Intellectum

In any case, what we affirmed above helps us to situate the phenomenon of "faith" in the rational sphere of man, as an event that concerns his cognitive sphere. Already these elementary considerations permit us to see how faith is not simply able to be relegated to the circle of irrationality or outside the confines of human knowledge.

It concerns reason; it is an event that attains to the intelligence of man in his relationship with reality, and is involved with all human freedom, including will and affectivity. It goes well beyond the simple trust that there can be with regard to a person or to a hypothetical ultimate and normative principle of reality. Faith feeds off reality—"it is not added from outside human knowing"[28]—but, thanks to the light that comes from intelligence, it knows and runs along the course of reality, gradually ascending reality's various levels, all the way up to the last level. *Intellectus quaerens fidem*, we can say along the lines of the encyclical *Fides et Ratio* of St. John Paul II, recalling this ascending movement of reason, that pushes it beyond its cognitive limits which can be validated toward that which allows it to transcend and surpass itself.

Still, however, it is the same Jesus—identified in the New Testament as the one who gave a beginning (*archegon*) to faith and brought it to fulfillment (*teleioten*)[29]—who invites us to understand how it is inherent in the way we consider the world and life: "When you see a cloud rising in the west, you say immediately that it is going to rain—and so it does; and when you notice that the wind is blowing from the south you say that it is going to be hot—and so it is. You hypocrites! You know how to interpret the appearance of the earth and the sky; why do you not know how to interpret the present time? Why do you not judge for yourselves what is right?" (Lk 12:54-57).

Therefore, faith begins to bring us within the comprehension of the real, which we see with our eyes, starting from that which takes place in this world. It embraces discerning, judging, and understanding what is in play in the reality in which one lives, from the most quotidian and apparently prosaic reality, to what concerns history and the final destinies of man and the world, opening passages to the ultimate foundation.

This discernment is the event that demands human intelligence—*fides quaerens intellectum*, as the great philosopher and theologian Anselm of Canterbury said—and regards it as an invitation to throw open its cognitive horizons, to amplify its perspectives, even to the point of comprehending the significance of that which occurs from the immediate to the very last. It is an act of profound knowledge of reality, and starts from that reality which we all know.

On the other hand, there are the Gospels—which offer us the *Magna Charta* of the events that concern the Christian faith—to present it to us in this way. In the Gospels, some people, encountering Jesus of Nazareth, familiarizing themselves with him, slowly recognize in that man—therefore, through a cognitive event—that by means of his gestures, his words, his countenance, he is revealed as far more. In that man, they recognize present and near to their life the Mystery that makes all things: he whom the religious tradition of humanity calls "God."

Associating with that man, with the help of his presence, words, and glances, their reason fulfills that passage which brings them to recognize in him, precisely in that man, God himself. They, with him, are led to fulfill, almost without being aware of it, that leap which human reason often holds as impossible and paradoxical: to recognize that the Universal makes itself present and comes to coincide in a particular historical person who is well identified. This, in fact, occurs when those who are nearest to him begin to recognize already in that man Jesus the one who, after his death and resurrection, will reveal himself to them as "Lord" and "God."[30] Therefore, for good reason, has Hans Urs von Balthasar defined Jesus Christ as "the concrete universal."

From the surprise of seeing him who changes water into wine at Cana in Galilee to the multiplication of loaves and fish, from the walking on the waters of Lake Tiberias to his reappearance alive after the bloody death on the ignominious gibbet of the Cross, a certainty arose from the reality that they knew and that was growing greater in their reason, becoming faith, profound conviction.

But perhaps the trajectory of this certainty is documented still more from the great encounters of Jesus that the Gospels narrate: from the paralytic to the man born blind, from the adulterous woman to the Samaritan woman, all the way to the good thief on the cross. Here, the experience of tenderness with which Jesus draws near— especially to derelicts, the weak, whoever was in need, and above all the mercy with which he drew near to sinners, pardoned them, and invited them to conversion—manifest in him such a human glance, so in measure with the human heart, as to reveal himself superhumanly capable of drawing near to the human heart completely.

That man is God: in him, the Old and the New Testament are joined together in covenant. In him are joined heaven and earth and, thanks to him, heaven—the foundation of reality, that otherwise would remain, even though desired, inaccessible to man— finally becomes "open." This is the certainty to which "the eyes of faith" lead.

Conversatus est cum hominibus—not only has he spoken in a human way with human beings, but he has dwelt as man in the midst of them—as the Latin version of the Bible says (Bar 3:38). "The invisible God out of the abundance of his love speaks to men as friends and lives among them, so that he may invite and take them into fellowship with himself. . . . By this revelation then, the deepest truth about God and the salvation of man shines out for our sake in Christ, who is both the mediator and the fullness of all revelation." This text from the Dogmatic Constitution of the Second Vatican Council, *Dei Verbum* (no. 2), is an echo of the Scriptures.

In the recognition of God, who in Jesus of Nazareth became man in the midst of men, and in adherence to him, one finds the heart of the Christian faith. Here we can detect a second movement—that, in truth, is possible only because of "the first" from the ontological point of view—a condescending movement of the Mystery, which is presented to the knowledge of man.

This is signified by the initial words of the First Letter of John: "What was from the beginning, what we have heard, what we have seen with our eyes, what we looked upon and touched with our hands concerns the Word of life—for the life was made visible; we have seen it and testify to it and proclaim to you the eternal life that was with the Father and was made visible to us" (1 Jn 1:1-2). Hearing, seeing, touching are verbs that describe the occurrence of faith in the man who, in Christ, recognizes God.

Logos and *Agape*: The Foundations of Reality at the Root of Faith, Hope, and Charity

In Jesus Christ is revealed to human beings the Word of life, who is the original *Logos*, the foundational principle of all things, the primordial reason and originator of the cosmos, the *mysterion* to which St. Paul makes reference in his letters.[31]

In that man, who gave his life "to the end" (Jn 13:1) for love of men, is revealed the universal salvific will of God toward all men[32]—this is precisely what invites us to profess the creed of the Christian faith, with the expression "*pro nobis*"—and it becomes clear that at the beginning of all things there is a profound nexus between rationality and love; therefore, the heart of reality, despite its contradictions, thanks to Jesus Christ, is revealed to be not a place of chaos and emptiness, but a space in which *Logos* and *Agape* are indistinguishably connected.

As the theologian Joseph Ratzinger, later Pope Benedict XVI, teaches us, in Jesus Christ, "the primacy of the Logos and the primacy of love proved to be identical. The Logos was seen to be, not merely a mathematical reason at the basis of all things, but a creative love taken to the point of becoming sympathy, suffering with the creature." In him, then, "in love and reason coming together as the two pillars of reality: the true reason is love, and love is the true reason. They are in their unity the true basis and the goal of all reality."[33]

Precisely because in Jesus Christ the true reason for reality is revealed to be love, and this weaving together of *logos* and *agape* becomes clear as the foundation and end of all that exists, one who lives in faith recognizes and welcomes this truth—even in the face of the grave contradictions that agitate the heart of man or that move life and the world—that man can finally "hope" and look to the present and the future with trust. This is so because the positivity that reveals itself in Jesus is discovered as the sign that expresses and communicates efficaciously the ultimate positivity from which everything comes and toward which everything goes, beyond every contrary appearance. The light of truth and goodness, of rationality and love that manifest themselves in Jesus Christ, spread out, as from a center, toward every life, toward history and the cosmos, revealing the positivity of their origin and purpose: "Christ is . . . all in all, he who holds all within himself according to the unique, infinite and most wise power of his goodness—as a center in which converge the lines—so that the creatures of God do not remain extraneous and inimical to each other but have a common place to manifest their friendship and peace."[34]

The positivity that man can encounter in Jesus Christ not only gives a new sense and decisive direction to his life,[35] but thanks to the light coming from his Resurrection, also becomes the hope before a great limit, before the great rock formation against which every human aspect and undertaking is smashed: death.

Hence, why the Tradition of the Church, from the beginning, has understood faith itself as a light that enlightens with positivity the life of men and of the entire world: *fides mundi lumen.* Therefore, in a reasonable and not blind way, not deaf to difficulties, to antinomies, and to dangers of every type that characterize human existence, the faith in Jesus Christ that the Church proclaims contains already in itself a hope. Faith, in fact, opens a positive light onto the future, precisely starting with the pledge of truth and goodness—a truth and goodness stronger than every limitation—that knows and receives from God in the present.

This pledge of truth and goodness, of *logos* and *agape*, that becomes accessible in Christ, invites us to a reasonable hope, filling the heart of man with gratitude for the gift received. Since there is here nothing that would push one to love like gratitude for a great love received, this gift moves man in its own turn from gratitude to love.[36] This love, first received from God and then given, takes the name of "charity."

Charity is, in fact, the life of man that becomes an operative action, thanks to faith in Jesus Christ and the sustaining help of his Spirit. It is gratitude toward God that becomes a gift, even to the total sacrifice of self, for love of one's brethren. There is, in fact, a sort of "squinting" congenital to the Christian faith. The more—in reality and not only in words or in a ritual formalism—man looks to God and allows himself to be looked at by him, so much the more does he become capable of regarding with familiarity even to the point of loving the one who stands next to him, who from being a stranger becomes a "neighbor." Here one is dealing with a love in action, which tends to share the needs of one's neighbor, inclines to accompany and to assist, and is not indifferent to the destinies of one's neighbors as to the destinies of those far away from him: in short, it is a love that tends to expand the dimensions of the human heart according to the dimensions of the heart of God.

Familiarity, love, and sharing give an operative substance to faith, which is called to be actualized, in hope, by means of charity: *fides quae per caritatem operatur*, as the letter of St. Paul reminds the Christians of Galatia (Gal 5:6). Therefore, faith is "intimately formed by love and brought to fulfillment in the eschatological sense by hope in eternal life"[37]: therefore, *fides, caritate et spe formata*.[38] Precisely this "form" of faith, fully actualized in man, is what, from the beginnings of the Church,[39] has more appealed to and convinced people concerning the truths she proclaims. This fascinating activity is nourished by an uninterrupted reciprocity between truth and love, which in its turn goes back to the original reciprocity between *Logos* and *Agape*, a reciprocity on which all reality is founded and with which it is impregnated.

Life in Christ as Life in Ecclesial Faith: "I, But No Longer I"

At this point, I would like to offer a subsequent mention concerning the very nature of faith and the implications that derive from it for one who welcomes it. Faith in its most profound substance is the relation of man with God "Our Father," who centers his revelation in Jesus Christ and perpetuates it, thanks to the gift of the Holy Spirit. Through faith we are made "sons of God" in his Only-Begotten Son.[40] Therefore, faith introduces man into communion with the Triune God, vitally placing him within the reciprocity of the *Logos* and *Agape*, which likewise reveal and manifest human nature, which is rational and relational. The same rational nature of man constitutes him as a being in relation in a particular way to the cosmos, to the point of allowing him to enter into a free and conscious relationship with the original *Logos*, and this is possible precisely because "his own reason, is *logos* of the one *logos*, thought of the original thought, of the creative spirit that permeates and governs his being."[41]

This free and conscious relationship with the "foundational" *Logos*—inscribed in human creatureliness and at the origin of the specific way by which man can relate to all other beings (although wounded and obscured as a result of the consequences of sin), thanks to inclusion in the Trinitarian life of the man who welcomes in his very depths this gift of God—receives a full appreciation, a deepening, and a connotation that are completely unheard of and completely personal.

In synthesis, we can say that there is a detonating event of this special intensification of the free and conscious relationship of man with God: it is the event of the Resurrection of Jesus Christ that, thanks to its diffusion carried out by the Spirit of Pentecost, opens itself to the universal and become accessible to all humanity.

Such an event values and deepens the constitutive and free ability to relate, which is inscribed in human nature, marking it as a relationship with God in Christ Jesus, through the gift of his Spirit. This means that the life of man becomes irrevocably—even if not removing it from highs and lows and from the unknown realities of human freedom—enclosed in a bond with God, a bond of filial intimacy that offers itself as an all-encompassing horizon of man's freedom of knowledge and of establishing oneself in the world. Therefore, if the faith begins and lives in the individual person, it cannot be actualized and realized in a radically autonomous subjectivity, but rather in the reciprocity of a communal "we."

"Insofar as I now live in the flesh, I live by faith in the Son of God who has loved me and given himself up for me" (Gal 2:20), explains St. Paul. Thanks to this inclusion, it is I who live, St. Paul says, but also at the same time, "Christ lives in me." "*I, but no longer I*," comments Pope Benedict XVI, explaining this Pauline text:

> With these words, Paul is not describing some mystical experience which could perhaps have been granted him, and could be of interest to us from a historical point of view, if at all. No, this phrase is an expression of what happened at Baptism. My "I" is taken away from me and is incorporated into a new and greater subject. This means that my "I" is back again, but now transformed, broken up, opened through incorporation into the other, in whom it acquires its new breadth of existence.

The pope continues:

> The great explosion of the Resurrection has seized us in Baptism so as to draw us on. Thus we are associated with a new dimension of life into which, amid the tribulations of our day, we are already in some way introduced. To live one's own life as a continual entry into this open space: this is the meaning of being baptized, of being Christian. This is the joy of the Easter Vigil. The Resurrection is not a thing of the past, the Resurrection has reached us and

44

seized us. We grasp hold of it, we grasp hold of the risen Lord, and we know that he holds us firmly even when our hands grow weak. We grasp hold of his hand, and thus we also hold on to one another's hands, and we become one single subject, not just one thing. *I, but no longer I*: this is the formula of Christian life rooted in Baptism, the formula of the Resurrection within time.[42]

Therefore, life lived in faith is removed from an individualistic solipsism and is made concrete in a new identity of an "I" related to a "we," whose body consists in the person of the Risen Christ and of those who have accepted to belong to him in the Sacrament of Baptism: this is the Church.

For this reason, Christian faith, if it wants to be faithful to what God himself has accomplished in Jesus Christ, cannot be anything but "ecclesial" faith. This is its authentic nature. "Ecclesial" faith signifies faith lived in this new subject that renders us "one" (*eis*) in him. "One," which is to say, one subject in which I myself certainly live, with my personal countenance, but one whose identity defines itself in relation to that new subjectivity, containing infinity and destined to recapitulate in itself the entire world (*anakefalaiosis*), who is the Risen Christ.

A New Glance and a New Action: Orthodoxy and Orthopraxis

This new identity concerns the ontology of man and is thus real; it tends to consider and express itself with a new glance and a new heart, in a movement that "shapes the whole of human existence according to the radical new reality of the resurrection. To the extent that he freely cooperates, man's thoughts and affections, mentality and conduct are slowly purified and transformed, on a journey that is never completely finished in this life. 'Faith working through love' (Gal 5:6) becomes a new criterion of understanding and action that changes the whole of man's life"[43] and renders it always more faithful to his being the image of God.

Therefore, if believing means adhering to God who reveals himself and thus, in some way and inchoatively, beginning to look at the world "with the eyes of God," such a glance is rendered present and real in every time by means of the glance of the risen body of Christ in the world, that is, of the Church. Hence, at this level—not ideological, nor collective in a depersonalizing and alienating sense—it is "the obedience of faith" (Rom 16:26). Although one would find human freedom often reticent, freedom is in reality immediately felt with this glance and with these new eyes that live in the Risen Christ and in his Body. It is a seeing and a thinking "according to Christ" and a seeing and a thinking of all things "in him."

Faith then implies an obedience which, if it is thus understood, does not harm freedom; neither is it supine or something that one endures, but it requires being assumed freely and demands a following that challenges, involves, and values all human freedom.

Christian faith invites one to an immediate experience with a living glance and a living heart, and in this faith is all the space for a dramatic dialogue, whether between the freedom of God and that of man, or between the respective freedoms of human beings.

Precisely at this level is found the necessary and inseparable relation between *orthodoxy* and *orthopraxis,* to which the Church calls attention. Precisely because this intensification moves at the same time reason and all of man's freedom, the adherence of faith, to which the new life in Christ calls, demands a coherence that is both *noetic* and *ethical.* Faith, in fact, generates a new behavior (*praxis*) from a new mentality (*nous*). St. Paul makes reference to the *sequela* of this newness when he describes life in the faith as being "obedient from the heart" (Rom 6:17), as "a being consigned to a form of particular teaching" (*typon didakes*), to that new "rule" of life and thought that flows from the Risen Christ and lives today in the heart of the Church. This is not a rigid alignment or constriction of freedom regarding some strategic taking of positions: it is a communion of life that certainly has a hierarchical structure, but whose substance and expression is always called to assume the demanding form of truth and love.

In this communion, human beings enter into familiarity with God and therefore cannot remain strangers to each other; letting themselves be taken by the hand by God, they are called to be taken by the hand and to accompany one another. In poetic fashion, the writer, Charles Péguy, expressed this familiarity and common pathway: "We are not saved on our own. No one returns to the house of the Father alone. Everyone gives his hand to another. The sinner extends his hand to the saint, and the saint extends his hand to Jesus." The *communio vitae* that comes from God does not leave man stagnant in his positions, but calls him to a continual exodus from himself toward horizons of humanity that are always growing: "on a journey never completely finished in this life."[44] It is a journey of the glance and of the heart, drawing along with it one's entire existence and tending to involve as companions along the way, in truth and in love, all those willing to be docile to the most noble aspirations of their spirit.

Thus, in every time and generation, documented and perpetuated is a new beginning of the Kingdom of God, that fullness (*pleroma*) of a new life that flows from the Resurrection of Christ and is spread abroad, thanks to his Spirit.

Christ, "Morning Star" and Light of Faith

We understand now in a more profound way what we said at the beginning regarding the light that comes from faith in Jesus Christ. It is a light that emanates from his risen humanity and that throws a beneficent and authentically human light onto our existence. In the darkness that the world can seem to us, especially in difficult historical periods, this light represents a secure orientation. The Book of Revelation alludes to Jesus as "the morning star" (Rev 2:28); this star announces the end of the night and the beginning of the dawn, the coming of a new day, and of a new season of time.

Opening our eyes to faith, we allow this light to invade our hearts with hope and to fill our hands with new works. Let us allow ourselves to let God take us by the hand, by his Son, Jesus; let us take each other by the hand and, well aware of our poverty, let us be led by this good light toward the new day that God never ceases to prepare for us.

II. "From the god of the dead to the God of the living"

Johann Wolfgang von Goethe loved to say: "Life is too short to drink bad wine": a curious adagio, in which is reflected the epicurean concept of the world and the nihilism almost infantile for its obstinacy, like many postmodern elites of the day.

With respect to such a position, the Christian vision of the world and of man resounds like a beautiful song to life and optimism. That is the optimism that St. Paul expresses with enthusiasm in the Letter to the Romans: "Rejoice in hope, endure in affliction, persevere in prayer. Contribute to the needs of the holy ones, exercise hospitality" (Rom 12:12-13).

It is a fact that the life of man on earth is brief, and the more his days pass, so much the more does each person perceive the *brevitas vitae* as an existential challenge. However, this is precisely the point: time is *the* resource given to us to rouse ourselves from the sleep of the ideology of self-realization or, said otherwise, from the pretense that man can build himself up, relying solely on his own forces. We could, therefore, repeat: "Life is too short to be weighed down with a bad philosophy." The Constitution, *Gaudium et Spes*, of the Second Vatican Council affirms this proposition: "In the face of the modern development of the world, the number constantly swells of the people who raise the most basic questions or recognize them with a new sharpness: What is man? What is this sense of sorrow, of evil, of death, which continues to exist despite so much progress? What purpose have these victories purchased at so high a cost? What can man offer to society, what can he expect from it? What follows this earthly life?"[45]

Atheism and "Neo-Atheism"

Atheism affirms that God does not exist. There's nothing new here. It is enough to recall the psalm of David that for three thousand years proclaims: "The fool says in his heart, 'There is no God'" (Ps 14:1). The most recent statistics attest to a dizzying increase of "converts" to atheism. Why do more and more people declare themselves to be atheists? Is atheism truly the most logical attitude, as atheists affirm? Why do books like *The Selfish Gene* or *The God Delusion* of Richard Dawkins or *God Is Not Great* of Christopher Hitchens figure on the best-seller lists?

Pope Benedict XVI, in his letter to the atheist mathematician, Piergiorgio Odifredi, affirmed that the "mimetic" theory of Richard Dawkins is simply a sci-fi proposal, worthy of "science *fiction*." In his works, Dawkins in fact maintains that, precisely as the genes in procreation transmit biological information, so too do the "copies," the "mimes," transmit the cultural formation by imitation. The ideas and opinions would pass, therefore, from mind to mind as invisible "copies," "mimes." But that is not enough: Dawkins uses a similar theory to criticize religion, from the angle that, in his judgment, religious beliefs are nothing more than "viruses" that infect a sick man.

Dr. Michael Blume, famous evolutionary biologist and theologian, has recently confirmed, on his part, that "the affirmation of Benedict XVI is absolutely pertinent": neither have the "copies," the "mimes," been able to be defined, despite numerous attempts undertaken in this regard, nor has it become possible to maintain that some type of serious study has verified them from an empirical and scientific point of view. On the contrary, while all the "mimetics" have already abandoned a similar theory since 2010, still today only Richard Dawkins has not yet said anything about its scientific failure.

How does one explain this fact? It is necessary not to forget that the justification offered by modern atheism about the process of de-Christianization of European and North American civilization, begun in the eighteenth century, and its subsequent proposal of a

49

hedonistic style of life imprinted by what is useful and profitable, pretends to realize itself through forms of science that have only an exterior garment.

The so-called "neo-atheism" does not offer any type of new foundations not already possible to find clearly formulated by David Hume and all those who from then until now have belonged and belong to the group of empiricists and materialists. Simply, one attempts, on the horizon of evolutionary theory and of neurophysiology, to extend the typical approach of the natural sciences—such as astrophysics, biology, and cerebrospinal research—which would determine a scientific vision of the world, and, according to the same pretension, one which is objective: all of this, without the awareness that such a consideration of man excludes his being taken as a "person," a subject responsible for his acts and capable of entertaining a personal relationship with God.

A similar pseudo-scientific vision of the world, propagandized by neo-atheism, comes down to our day exalted as a program of opinion to be imposed on all of humanity. Carried to its extreme, such a theory argues that, if someone believes in the existence of a personal God, such a person must not be granted the right of existence either in the world of culture—having thus contracted the "divine virus" and needing therefore to be quarantined—or of citizenship in the same natural world of men, for being judged a social parasite.

The intolerant and inhuman character of neo-atheism becomes even more evident if we consider political atheism as it was historically planned by national socialism in Germany, or by the Stalinist program of extinction of the Church as it was achieved in the former Soviet Union. So-called "scientific atheism" intends, therefore, always to impose itself as a global vision of the world and, through its intrinsic characteristics, as a totalitarian political program of absolute inhumanity.

At the beginning of the modern epoch, one finds the opposition between empiricism and rationalism and with it the attempt to resolve the dualism in favor of one of the two ways of having access to reality. Can thought appropriate the material world? Or is it precisely the reverse, that reason is always a function of the evolutionary process? Is man, as a thinking subject, only a part of the moment of the differentiation of matter, submitted to the law of natural selection as any other product, deprived of substance, part of an integral totality that encompasses everything?

Robert Spaemann has well synthesized the concept of *modernity* in its negative repercussions on man as a person, which person is gifted with his own moral and intellectual capabilities: "The scientific vision of the world steals the '*I*' and the '*you*' from the brief life of the individual, from his complexity and significance, from being the unique representation of the unconditioned, to the advantage of a collective development, which is in itself like the only truthful bearer of meaning."[46] The typical approach of modernity has its root in the empiricism of David Hume, according to whom, "we are never able to go beyond ourselves."[47] It is necessary to underscore that a similar reductionist vision does not take into consideration the evident capacity of the intellect to go "beyond" with respect to what appears immediately.

The discoveries of the recent research of an evolutionary type and of neurobiology are little concerned with the essential structure of man as a being gifted with a corporal and spiritual nature and with an inclination toward the knowledge of the truth and of the good and, therefore, toward full personal realization.

Such research is limited to considering the material conditions of reason and of the acts of the will of man from the point of view of a pseudo-scientific interpretation that imposes itself as a philosophy that is marked by a monistic materialism. Given its tendency to be converted into a monism of an idealist type, the true project of modernity, with its undeniable humanizing value, will be able to reach its goal only when it overcomes the presupposition of empiricism and its derivatives of materialism, positivism, and rationalism.

"Lord, what is man that you are mindful of him?" (Ps 8:5)

If we want to define man in his fullness, we cannot limit ourselves to considering him as the mere object of research conducted on nature, history, culture, and morality, since he always remains the one capable of conducting a knowing reflection on himself. Man, as a being placed in space and in time, cannot deny sensible mediation in the material and sociological context, which sustains the material conditions of his existence. Nevertheless, to guarantee both the project of individual liberty in relation to the collectivity, and personal awareness with respect to a merely positive law, as well as the inalienable dignity of every human being with respect to the instrumentalization of the interests of the group (class, people, capital, etc.), a *metaphysics of reality* and an *anthropology of the transcendence* of man are indispensable, putting him in relationship to the source of creation.

A metaphysics of being and of knowledge of God, in the sense specifically elaborated by philosophical theology, is not of merely historical interest, but is the condition to ensure that the project of modernity does not get shipwrecked into a sterile dialectic of the Enlightenment. Not for nothing has the dialogue with human reason been a more important dialogue than the one with religions, from the beginning of Christianity until our days: only thus, in fact, is an integral access to reality gained and, consequently, the possibility of elaborating an effective natural theology.

This does not mean a return to a past form of metaphysics in the face of the proposal that the natural sciences and the philosophical reflection that flows from modernity offer to mundane reality: neither to demonstrate the reasonableness of our approach, nor even less to justify the contents of the supernatural revelation of God in Jesus Christ. Rather, starting with the experience of the real world, one is dealing with the intention of reaching a reflective self-understanding that being a "spirit" makes man possible, and attaining to a knowledge of God, not as he is in himself, but insofar as the world exists in relation to him, who is the origin and end of all finite being, including man. Man recognizes himself as a person only in the light of such a transcendent orientation. When he searches for truth and tends toward the good, then it is in God that man encounters peace.

Therefore, discourse on God cannot begin from his pure being in himself, as if we could abstract God from the existing world. If finite and creaturely reason always begins from the experience of the world that already exists, the affirmation of "God" is here to mean the point of provenance of being and spirit, without however reducing it to a type of mundane object known only in an accessory way. Insofar as he is a principle (of knowledge), man is constitutively determined as a spirit precisely for the inevitable and unavoidable reference to God. A *posteriori*, one must be conscious of such an *a priori* and transcendent moment of his own realization: only thus does God appear as the uncircumscribed horizon toward whom we move and from whom we know we have come in an absolute sense, without converting him into a categorical objective. The spirit transcends itself intentionally only if it directs itself toward the infinite, only if it recognizes itself constituted in its intentionality by the absolute extra-mundane reality of God. One understands this in the final analysis only by means of the *reality* of the transcendent God.

Using the words of St. John of the Cross: "When Thou didst regard me, Thine eyes imprinted in me Thy grace. . . . Since Thou hast regarded me, Grace and beauty hast Thou given me."[48] We conceive the concept of "God" as the real condition of our spiritual being in the world and therefore also as the condition of our finite reality. While the essence of God is the absolute possession of the act of being, the world and finite reality exist by means of the reception of the act of being under the form of participation. The world participates in the being of God, inasmuch as it exists by the will of God, precisely in the form of finite being. On the contrary, God exists through himself and in himself by virtue of himself and by his proper reality.[49] He is *ipsum esse per se subsistens*.[50]

The spiritual nature of man, for its part, is the principle that renders finite and concrete the way of man's participation in the spiritual being of God. God, meanwhile, as Spirit is directly given to himself and can similarly share of himself, of his spiritual act of being. This means that spirit constitutively forms a part of the very structure of the origin of being. This relation with God, even where

53

it does not manage to express itself in a thematic mode, constitutes "existence-in-itself," the presupposition and condition of what we call "personal being."

The creative action of God is the permanent insertion of the world in God and its realization through God. For this reason, no contradiction exists between the affirmation of creation by means of the *Logos* and the sustaining which the Creator *Logos* offers to all things in the process of their evolution. In man, the natural history of being goes beyond into the history of spirit and, therefore, man cannot but conceive himself as the perfect spiritual reception of real being by his essence, in which he exists as a person: that is, a being-in-itself. The transcendence of the created person toward participation in the spiritual reality of God is possible because creation is, implicitly, the self-manifestation of the being and goodness of God. The creation of being and of finite spirit indicates the openness to an unlimited horizon for the explicit manifestation of God in his word. Or, said otherwise, the Creator of the world, of nature, and of man encounters man in a personal way as the fulfillment of his self-transcendence: that which determines the created spirit, drawn in by the uncreated Spirit.

The unique, atemporal, and indivisible act of creation coincides, beyond created things, with the actuality of God. To the extent that infinite actuality of being is realized in a finite way in created things, these do not adequately belong to the divine self-illumination; but to the extent that they participate in the being of God, they are creaturely means by which we come to know and love God. The knowledge and love of God manifest themselves in the most profound way as a creaturely participation in the self-knowledge of God. For this reason, the creaturely realization of a created spirit is nothing else but an *event*, in which God himself makes himself known and loved. Thus we read in Romans 1:19-20: "For what can be known about God is evident to them, because God made it evident to them. Ever since the creation of the world, his invisible attributes of eternal power and divinity have been able to be understood and perceived in what he has made." And in Acts 17:26-28: "He made from one the whole human race to dwell on the entire surface of the earth, and he fixed the ordered seasons and boundaries of their regions, so that people might seek God, even perhaps grope for him and find him, though indeed he is not far from any one of us. For 'In him we live and move and have our being.'"

Concretely, man does not exist in a type of abstract effectivity from existence, but always in his concrete realization as a dynamic movement that tends to find itself completed in the other. Hence, we call "nature" the abstract separation of the simple constitution (*perfectio formae*) with respect to its effective realization (*operatio in perfectionem finis*). However, inasmuch as this nature is characterized by a movement toward God and toward the fulfillment of God's work, we speak of *grace*. If in man's realization as freedom and spirit, he distances himself from God, he loses grace and falls into fault (*defectus gratiae*). Before sin and distance from God, the permanent salvific presence of God assumes in man the character of *redemption*. The creative actuality of God, through which the creature exists, is thus revealed as pardon and reconciliation. In his Redeemer, the sinner encounters his Creator.

The original presence of the grace of God in creation, in its realization, and in the midst of creaturely realities, renders itself once again accessible under the form of *the grace of Jesus Christ*. In the eternal Word incarnate of God and in the Holy Spirit of God poured forth into hearts, the justified participate in the self-revelation of the One and Triune God, and thus, in this history of salvation, are rendered present in the world. The creative activity of God in the Word that reaches us in the form of redemption assumes directly in Jesus a creaturely reality. In Jesus, the sinner encounters a creaturely means made totally his own by God, a means that puts him into direct contact with the Creator as God the Redeemer. In this way, Jesus comes to be the fulfillment, the redemption, and the foundation that recreates spiritual nature and its self-transcendence mediated in a creaturely manner toward immediate nearness to God.

The transcendence and immanence of God stand in inverse proportionality. Only because God is absolutely transcendent with respect to the world can he be immanent in the world in an unsurpassable way. The conservation of the world (*creatio continua*), therefore, is not conceived as a series of singular creative acts, but consists in the atemporal and indivisible presence of the creative actuality of the existence and movement of the world. God is the uncreated and universal *causa prima*, who does not nullify the creaturely *causae secundae* of form, matter, causality, and finality; rather, he renders them capable of operating autonomously as only he is capable of doing. The "intervention" of God in the world can never signify a suspension of creaturely causality. God can, however, make creaturely causality the instrumental cause of his specific salvific will concerning man, of that man who possesses freedom as a concrete form of his existence. Man, therefore, not only has, but moreover *is*, spirit and freedom, although only in a finite way. The acts of God's self-revelation in his speaking and acting for the salvation of man are realized in the world, but not by means of created causality. Rather, they come to be known by man through the Word and the divine Spirit.

Since the transcendent God moves everything precisely according to the created nature of every finite being, he also moves man in conformity with his spiritual free nature. Predestination does not eliminate freedom, but enables man to do the universal salvific will by acceptance in faith of the principle of the self-movement of the spirit toward the promised end.

The relationship between the absolute production of man, his freedom activated by God, and the spiritual self-movement of man that constitutes his freedom, could be expressed thus: God does not exercise any *physically measurable* influence on created freedom, encountering it rather as a *motive* (*movens*) of its action. God, when he comes to me freely in the divine Word that manifests him, always actualizes himself as the fulfillment of my freedom: God and his freedom permit a dynamic movement of creaturely freedom to realize itself fully beyond its creaturely limits. Man, for whom God has become the *motive* of his action and self-projection in the world, knows that he is, in biblical terms, a type of "clay in the hands of the Creator who molds it." As a result, he says and confesses that God accomplishes in him his will and work.[51] At the same time,

56

however, he does not see himself deprived of his proper freedom and personality. On the contrary, he experiences himself rather as enabled to actuate his own freedom, and as he actualizes it, he knows that only thanks to the self-donation of God as fulfillment of his freedom is he able to act in view of his proper end. Actualization moves toward its end through the direct presence of the end itself: by grace, freedom is made capable of receiving, by self-actualization, its acceptance by God. In grace, God reveals himself as the eternal font of created freedom and as its eternal horizon under the form of love. The form of human freedom, then, is not realized in opposition to God, as atheism would like it, but only on the basis of the perfect spiritual freedom of God. If God is exalted, man is also exalted as a consequence. The salvation of man can only arrive from God who freely offers his grace to man.

St. Paul writes: "For by grace you have been saved through faith, and this is not from you; it is the gift of God; it is not from works, so no one may boast. For we are his handiwork, created in Christ Jesus for the good works that God has prepared in advance, that we should live in them" (Eph 2:8-10).

Along these lines, the Second Vatican Council teaches: "The Church firmly believes that Christ, who died and was raised up for all, can through his Spirit offer man the light and the strength to measure up to his supreme destiny. Nor has any other name under the heaven been given to man by which it is fitting for him to be saved. She likewise holds that in her most benign Lord and Master can be found the key, the focal point and the goal of man, as well as of all human history."[52]

Those who deny the metaphysical character of natural theology and therefore the possibility of the knowledge of God through Revelation, tend to fall into various forms of pessimism, often of a nihilistic or cynical type. The vision of the Church, instead, attains to this fullness that, through the grace of Jesus Christ, we have all received.[53] If Christ alone is "the true vine" (Jn 15:1), who offers "the good wine" (Jn 2:10) necessary for eternal life, we can then conclude that the Church alone is the true promoter of "modernity," given that only openness to God, the future of man, renders authentically possible for all precisely that hope which the Church never ceases to proclaim.

III. Contemporary Challenges for Theology

Mundus Reconcilatus, Mundum Reconcilians

All of us who have worked or who presently work, by whatever way or title, in the sphere of "theological" institutes, feel like we live a double tension on our "skin": on the one hand, we belong to a sphere of academia or research born within the *ecclesial milieu*, which, above all, intends to serve; on the other hand, we are, at the same time, also citizens of this world, of a human sphere toward which we are "debtors" precisely because we are citizens *in Ecclesia*: that is, precisely on account of the ecclesial nature of that sphere in which and starting from which our thought and reflection are constitutively called to be born and to develop.

In fact, the Church is both *mundus reconciliatus*[54] and *mundus reconcilians mundum*.[55] On the other hand, it is the "paradoxical" condition in which every Christian "citizen" finds himself, the condition proper to the *Christifidelis* of all times, as the Letter to Diognetus reminds us: "Christians are indistinguishable from other men either by nationality, language or customs. They do not inhabit separate cities of their own, or speak a strange dialect, or follow some outlandish way of life. Their teaching is not based upon reveries inspired by the curiosity of men. Unlike some other people, they champion no purely human doctrine. With regard to dress, food and manner of life in general, they follow the customs of whatever city they happen to be living in, whether it is Greek or foreign."

The Church lives simultaneously in two dimensions, belonging to the time and space of that reconciliation with God that has already occurred and in that other time and space in which such reconciliation is not yet present. From here, a double tension comes about: the tension to discover how God has already reconciled to himself the person who lives in the Church, and the tension to recognize how this reconciliation is offered today to the persons who live around us. Between these two tensions, our work as scholars of theology is called to situate itself.

Thanks to the movement born from the first tension, theology enlightens the divine and the human with all their meaning, to offer them—and we are here already in the movement that springs forth from the second tension—the humble strength of witness to the world. Here we are concerned with two movements involved with one another, not consecutive but in a certain sense contemporaneous, even if they maintain a certain *taxis* or hierarchy. Theology is faithful to itself when it respects and develops all the meaning and breadth of these two movements, whose direction attains to the Revelation of God to enlarge the horizon of the human.

What is the human and cultural context in which this double movement takes place today? I do not want so much to engage in a point by point review, with a so-called "academic" rigor, the names and currents of thought that particularly characterize it as much as to recall, in a somewhat abbreviated form, the major instances that identify our contemporary existence, positively and negatively, both as a possibility and as a danger. These are merely hints, not intended to define but only to open passages for an easier understanding, and by which I would like to stimulate a deeper dialogue. To deepen, first of all, those perspectives that today open themselves up to faith, which recognizes the gifts received—and for which it is responsible—to contribute to the edification of the generations in the midst of which we find ourselves and which have been entrusted to us.

Discernment, History, Hope

There are three traits that in broad strokes, among many, mark out contemporary Western man in a particular way.

1. Contemporary man, living in the so-called "Western society," since he is inserted into a world that is always more "global" and rich in communications, becomes pressed, as never before, by an

intense nearness to others. Each one of us understands the immense possibility that this represents. Nevertheless, we note at the same time that today man lives a proximity always more occasional, on account of his incapacity/refusal to forge solid bonds, and tends to present himself ever more as a self-referential subject, individualizing and realizing himself.

This absence of stable bonds makes him ever more fragile and places him in the power of the contexts in which he moves, ever less capable of discerning critically what would enhance or lessen the dignity of his own human being, ever more set to sound every useful possibility presented to him. Man today is no longer capable of forms of discernment that transcend the short breath of what is useful and immediate: he no longer recognizes what corresponds to or what repels the unique elements that render him truly human.

We understand, therefore, that, in this perspective, the depth of the culture produced by him becomes ever thinner: a culture which is as powerful in the instruments and technology of communication as it is poor, humanly speaking, in the contents communicated. A culture in which what appears significant does not transcend the confines of the *short term* and of the *cheap*. An effective metaphor of this is the velocity with which the media today burn up news and images, in a vortex of communication. The more one communicates, the more the quantity of the facts communicated multiplies, so much the less do we enter into genuine communication with one another. And the quality of the communication ends by reducing itself to a technical affair of *bites* and *pixels*. Everything develops and is refined around coordinates of standardized procedures, or protocols, that ever more hasten to guarantee only the form of the relations. "So much more" and "so much less" are the refrain with which we can often define the reciprocal forward movement of technology and the backward movement of humanity. A new Narcissus, man: the more he looks at the image of himself which he produces, the more he becomes proud of the work of his hands, so much the less does he rediscover his own countenance, ending up by seeing himself drowned, in his own images, which pertain indelibly to his *humanum*.

2. In the second place, the average citizen of the postmodern era, precisely because he is evaluated on the basis of fragile relations and is ever less a forger of significance, struggles to perceive his being as inserted in a "history." The more the horizon of man empties itself of pregnant meanings, the less is he capable of understanding time as a propitious occasion, as *kairos*, as history. The more that not only the horizontal bonds of proximity but also those vertical bonds with the generations that precede him and with those that follow him are peeled off—this is the bitter fruit which comes from the dissolution of the family as the place of generations of solid and indissoluble bonds—so much the less does he see himself inserted into a history.

The significance of time says "identity" and "bonds," which in their turn interlace with the flow of days into events and visages, making it "history": that is, the construction of personal and particular histories as universal and global ones. And the more the time that passes comes to be seen as being followed up by events significant for man, so much the more is his freedom perceived as called upon and challenged by the passing days, which are not spent ineluctably or in vain.

On the contrary, the absence of a "history" produces, as a consequence, even a devaluation of the specific weight of human freedom, of this powerful instrument that is given to us as the possibility to carve out our destiny and that of the world. In this regard, we think of the lack of confidence which so many young people today have in their ability to change the world in which they live: as human beings, they are endowed in their proper nature with the powerful instrument of freedom; however, since they are not educated to recognize its full power and to practice it in its proper sense, they are skeptical about its potentialities.

3. The two preceding traits, which I recalled above with a quick sketch, also introduce another characteristic that today marks the majority of our contemporaries. It is this element to which Pope Francis often calls our attention: it is a difficulty to look to the future with trust, with hope, knowing how to keep in one's heart *"the ideals of youth,"* as St. John XXIII would say. To the extent that significant

relations in the present are fed or fade, the other two dimensions of time likewise lose their weight and rise up against one another, filling the life of man with an *"unsustainable lightness of being"*: the past becomes a series of antecedents that tend to influence it in a deterministic and mechanistic way, while the future is shortened and surrounded by obscurity.

Thus, it is difficult "to hope," to have trust in the very possibility that "positive" changes can come about: behind us there are enormous cogs holding us back while, before us, there is the darkness of uncertainty. For only where human freedom is weighty with significant relations—for good reason, did your Archbishop of many years repeat that it is right to speak of a human subject only as an *"I-in-relation"*—and becomes capable of discerning in the history of his action that which is good from that which is bad, only then is hope viable, only then is it possible to nourish a "trustworthy" hope, as Pope Benedict XVI often reminded us. Only then is it possible to act while also looking to the long term, thinking reasonably about a development that is truly "sustainable," and to sustain sacrifices that do not look only to immediate gains.

Discernment, history, and hope are the first and elementary contributions that faith—first of all through the practice of a life that witnesses to it and then also by means of a theological reflection that highlights its essential traits point by point—is called to offer to the world, in order to raise up again the fate of a humanity ever poorer in regard to relationships, meaning, and trust.

Here theology can give much to the *saeculum*, ever more *"brief,"* from which we come and in which we still find ourselves. Here we notice also the importance of the exercise of a reason that is both humble and strong, to which theology can bear witness as a positive occasion for rediscovering a reasonable orientation in the complexity of reality. There cannot in fact be a real discernment without a reason that is sure to find the truth: in a way that is neither exhaustive nor ideological, but counting profoundly upon the capacity of human freedom as healed and elevated.

There can be no real progress for man if he does not become certain of being able to attain to meanings that exceed those offered by the so-called "exact" sciences. If there is no confidence to look with hope to the future that awaits us, it is not possible to free up the energies and dynamics that would be effective in bringing about a change. There cannot be hope without certainty of finding the good: here also with modalities that are both certain and at the same time relatively reformable on the revealed front. From here, existentially, we can gather almost empirically how much the bond of freedom/truth/good is indissolubly connected with the binomium of hope-*dynamis*: these stand or fall together.

We think of all that becomes concrete against the background of that crisis which for some time has ensnared us: an anthropological crisis even before it is an economic and financial one; a crisis that demands radical responses, of that radicalism which only a profound change of the *humanum* can obtain; a crisis that awaits a cultural and *noetic* change even before that of structures and customs.

In this regard, precisely the experience of the human offered to us in the ecclesial context—where it is lived authentically—shows us how every reform that does not begin from the *nous* of man is destined to gather up and feed delusions and skepticism on the ethical side of things. We think of so many proposals of structural reforms that we feel today, which—although necessary and advantageous if taken in their secondary and penultimate nature—never bring about a decisive change. This is so because they are limited to the change of structures—a deep net of social ideologies by now outdated and surpassed by history—never drawing from the ultimate foundations of man: and if the change does not arrive there, it will never arrive.

Pluralistic Society, *Sensus Fidei*, Communication of Knowledge, Expanded Rationality

At this point, I would like to focus briefly on some current situations, whose summons we must feel.

1. Above all, the so-called "*pluralistic society*," in which we increasingly live: a society which is multiethnic, multicultural,

multireligious, multi-contextual. This plurality of contexts and subjects demands—he who has been guiding you with an effective synthesis for quite some time notes this likewise—that our work be expressed in an always less amateurish and self-referential language. It is unfortunately the habit of many of our academic environments to formulate their own knowledge with an excessive "code" language: even if not always necessarily, a cryptic one. On the one hand, there is a demand for linguistic rigor and depth in expressing complex contents that cannot go too far in simplification, so as to risk the impoverishment of the contents. On the other hand, there is, however, also the need to know how to communicate and translate, without betraying the theological data according to coordinates that are more accessible to the culture and subjects with whom we live, lest walls of alienation be erected instead of creating nearness, about which Pope Francis has strongly reminded us many times.

In this sense, I maintain that an example that has not been surpassed and is still to be fully appreciated is the thought of Pope Benedict XVI, whose magisterium is a luminous reference for the way he knew how to bring together profundity of thought and simplicity of language.

The question of the cultural "pluralism" in which we are immersed undoubtedly represents a stimulating challenge for "speaking" of faith in an understandable way, even to spheres distant from ours in terms of background and premises of thought and customs. With trust, we confront this challenge which forces us to negotiate difficult terrain with the humility of one who knows that he must proceed with caution and must be bold at the same time. In this regard, the critical rigor of theology must above all clear the field of the superficiality of one who allows himself to favor truisms created by the pressure of the media and of mentalities not compatible with the authentic contents of the faith: we are thinking of so much lightness in theologizing concerning themes like women's ordination, authority in the Church, access to the sacraments on the part of those not in full communion with the Church, and looking at this case, how much applause there is on the part of the media for certain theologians and theological opinions not rooted deeply in the essential doctrines of the faith. In this sense, there is today more than ever the risk of a sentimental drift from faith around certain themes, even at the level of theological expression. *Logos* and *Agape*, which are inseparable coordinates of being human in the world, are often opposed to one another, and often a love that is badly understood is used to obfuscate, if not to block out, the truth.

Hence, the still proper reminders about: the hierarchy of truths; the necessary multiform reality that is the very "catholic" nature that the Church demands; the unity of research above all around the essential elements of faith; the freedom to think, understood not as a pretext for an unacceptable autonomy. These do not eliminate the risk that every discourse runs of being vain if a previous question is not placed in focus: that of the *sensus fidei* and the *sensus fidelium* in the *Ecclesia*.

All of us understand that every debate in the Church avoids sterility and becomes fruitful only if it occurs within an authentic sense of faith, which can never be taken for granted. In this sense, every protagonist who wants to be such, within legitimate theological debates, must first of all authenticate his positions, especially if seeking to establish himself with an accent of novelty, witnessing above all to a substantial fidelity to the living transmission of the apostolic faith, whose fonts—Scripture, Tradition, and Magisterium—cannot be surpassed and twisted around.

In this sense, starting from here and never from anywhere else, do we understand that theology is a question not of individuals—professors, pastors, opinion groups—but, in a profound and truly theological sense, is a question "of the Church"; it is a reality that belongs to all who bear witness to a real *sensus fidei et Ecclesiae*, since there is no Church without the apostolic faith and there is no apostolic faith outside the sources that "make up" the Church.

Here, the words of Karl Barth appear unsurpassed and ever current, since in them we see in a filigree so much of what has already taken place in the many centuries of the history of the Church:

> Theology is not a private subject for theologians only. Nor is it a private subject for professors. Fortunately, there have always been pastors who have understood more about theology than most professors. Nor is theology a private subject of study for pastors. Fortunately, there have repeatedly been congregation members, and often whole congregations, who have pursued theology energetically while their pastors were theological infants or barbarians. Theology is a matter for the Church. (K. Barth, *Iniziare dall'inizio* [Brescia: Queriniana, 1991], 18)

All of this puts the question of faith at the center of our attention: it is precisely about this that Pope Benedict XVI wanted to remind us by inaugurating the *Year of Faith*. Therefore, there can be no purity of ecclesial service without a faith that is integral in its contents and integral in its expression. There can be no fruitful ecclesial service when faith is not faithful to itself, when it chooses methods that do not respect its fundamental heuristics, or when it is expressed by omitting or tampering with some of its essential elements, however that might be.

2. In this sense, a renewed reflection on the authentic contours of *sensus fidei, sensus fidelium, sensus Ecclesiae* is needed more than ever. Here theology today can and must give more, and there is no one who does not see the incorrectness and myopia of the use of e-mailing to sound indiscriminately through the Internet the opinion of the many. Very different are the fora and the agora that the Church today needs to recover and express, in an authentic way, that *sensus fidei* by which it is invigorated and rejuvenated in every age.

To have substituted the opinion of the internet for the proper places of the *sensus fidelium* reveals not only a *misunderstanding* about what constitutes the Church, but even leads one to think that some technologies of political pressure are retained in ecclesial formation, as more effective than the mutual criteria of the faith itself. When faced with the danger that politics counts more than faith even in the Church, theology today has an irreplaceable prophetic task: a task that today, more than ever, is prophetic and "the cause of martyrdom," in the literal sense of *martyria*.

In this regard, we look to that vast field of witness that opens before us, in a time when it is necessary to help our contemporaries—afflicted by a chronic misunderstanding of human freedom, and who use the lemma of *gender* to affirm themselves—to settle accounts with a substratum that cannot be turned around, pre-constituting every man. The concept of "nature," in fact, represents that fundamental *sine qua non*, without which man would not succeed in fixing, beyond the slippery and fickle contours of the majority of every age, the non-negotiable confines of his dignity and identity and, therefore, of his rights and obligations. These are a dignity and identity that are "given" to man, which man is called first to recognize and then to actualize, and which no one can invent without risking the loss of that identity and dignity, and of misunderstanding those rights and obligations: which is precisely what has taken place today and is happening still. Here too we await from theological reflection a contribution for which there is no substitute and that today also demands prophetic courage in the face of the continual attempts to manipulate human nature, identity, and life.

On the other hand, only if man succeeds in recovering fundamental and unconditioned absolutes for his own positioning in the world can he succeed in creating a dyke against the god of profit that seems to dominate all and to attract everyone, putting aside every form of knowledge that is not useful to it. Nussbaum, in fact, has denounced the danger that in the immediate future would assist in the *"production"*—we are not speaking here about "formation," but this is a point that I would like to highlight later—of generations of men, who only with grave difficulty will be capable of discerning what is human and worthy of man and what is not.[57]

In this sense, only ecclesial social doctrine can help law and economics recognize the original link between profit and solidarity, which sin tends to break and which a refound vision of unity that cannot be separated from the personal and common good allows to recompose. The common and personal good, in a demanding perspective and one that is responsible for subsidiarity, are called to work in synergy to safeguard the dignity and possession of the social fabric. These are only reminders that, in a rhapsodic way, permit me to formulate and to attempt to open useful ways to the theme you have entrusted to me.

3. There is then another question that I would like to bring to your attention. I would like to start here with a simple point: never before as in modernity has the importance been underscored and our attention called to the "subject" of freedom, its autonomy, its weight within epistemology. However, what have we witnessed in the so-called postmodern era? We have witnessed a sort of obscuring of the subject, at the price of an emphasis placed on the products of man's hands: man himself has been remade and become an object and product of his own action. Knowledge has also lost its profoundly "personal" character—that is, its connotation of communication among persons—in order to become a sort of remade vehicle of data.

Thus today, in the academic and scientific world, one speaks of "production of knowledge"; one maintains still that knowledge can be so objectified as to be almost a product to exchange among subjects, independently of their own being. Nevertheless, this is not what happens when knowledge is transmitted. In fact, every production and transmission of knowledge is not merely a communication of data, since it is also and inseparably, whether one wants to admit it or not, a communication of values, of a vision of man, and of the world. Among other things, this last is a communication that does not come about without consequences and does not remain indifferent to either the one who communicates or to those to whom it is communicated.

Here we are thinking of so much that is fraught with implications, if taken as data capable of rendering an accurate account, especially from an educational perspective. This, for example, means that there does not exist a form of teaching that is not formation at the same time. A teaching that would pretend to be free of formative demands falsifies, or at the very least ignores what occurs in the very human phenomenon of the communication of knowledge. This reality is made explicit and is assumed responsibly all the way to the end. Concretely, this means that every teacher must assume with full responsibility that process by which transmitting knowledge likewise communicates a horizon of values to his students. This fact means that every teacher—contrary to common practice and even though it would represent a serious task in every way—cannot be disinterested in the formation of his students or consider his teaching extraneous to it. Hence, why one cannot communicate well if, deep down, one does not take responsibility for those to whom one is communicating: that is, if one does not "love" those who are receiving one's message. This is something to which Pope Francis is continually bearing witness to us with his own person and action.

In this sense, also on this level, one detects around one a loss of the foundations that constitute the human. Man today knows many things about the biological, psychological, and sociological mechanisms of his communication but, having lost "the contours" of the identity of his "I," has lost the awareness of what profoundly occurs when an "I" communicates with another "I." Since the rationality of the *Logos* is snubbed as sub-scientific, the intrinsic cultural value of human communication is lost. Likewise here, a reason enlightened by faith is called to broaden the horizons of rationality of our contemporaries.

4. I maintain, therefore, that the appeal formulated by Pope Benedict XVI and stretched "to broaden the boundaries of rationality" is still all to be gathered together, sounded, and relaunched. Still we suffer the consequences of modern epistemology and the "new science," which have reduced—a great deal, by Galileo and later by Descartes—reason to its analytical faculties, thus compromising also its congenital openness to the transcendent. But without such openness, man loses the sense of his profound dignity and vocation, as the Second Vatican Council reminds us (see *Gaudium et Spes*, no. 21), precluding the possibility of knowing his eternal destiny. Similarly, without welcoming such an openness as an essential and

inescapable element of his reason, man also becomes a stranger to the dimensions and reasons which are inscribed indelibly on his heart—beauty, truth, justice—and which constitute the ultimate propelling force of his activity. Without understanding such dimensions, no one will ever understand man in the full meaning of his being and working in the world. Here theology still has much to say and to offer to contemporary thought.

Precisely starting from here, in fact, the Church can reveal efficaciously to man how the gift of which she is the bearer—the new life revealed and offered by God in Christ and in his Spirit—does not limit man and does not destroy his joy of living, but amplifies without end his horizons and opens up to him the prospect of a definitive reality, of something that will be "forever," without which every human gain is illusory and false.

These are only some points that I would like to offer for your reflection and about which it would likewise be interesting to open a conversation. Still other instances of thought and of the contemporary *ethos* confront our faith, challenging it to a relationship that would be rigorously critical and engaged in dialogue: in this lecture, I intend only to open some spaces and to offer a convinced opinion, in the hope of offering a small contribution. Permit me to make it precisely in the name of that "paradoxical citizenship" in which we have located our particular identity as the baptized, *Christifideles* people to whom, although living in the condition of all, it is given to live "by faith in the Son of God" (see Gal 2:20) that daily calls us, offers itself to us as a gift, and sends us to our contemporaries.

The "paradox" of this citizenship is an indelible trait of our placement in the world and generates a movement in which differences do not annul identities but continually put them in play, so that they might be purified and recomposed in a "catholic" embrace: one which shortens distances, generates real proximity, and knows how to identify ways to achieve a unity that is never in decline or cheap. Precisely at this level are we given the opportunity to appreciate the unbreakable bond between faith and truth, a nexus that we are called to highlight in every aspect of our work as "theologians." Wherever the faith is lived in its fullness, the world is always enlightened with the light of truth.

A pilgrimage in the truth is not an intellectual game.

Therefore, allow me to conclude by making my own some words of Pope Benedict XVI, words that I feel are ever more important and decisive for our work as theologians:

> Today the idea of truth and that of intolerance are almost completely fused, and so we no longer dare to believe in the truth or to speak of the truth. It seems to be far away, it seems something better not to refer to. No one can say: I have the truth—this is the objection raised—and, rightly so, no one can have the truth. It is the truth that possesses us, it is a living thing! We do not possess it but are held by it. Only if we allow ourselves to be guided and moved by the truth, do we remain in it. Only if we are, with it and in it, pilgrims of truth, then it is in us and for us. I think that we need to learn anew about "not-having-the-truth." Just as no one can say: I have children—they are not our possession, they are a gift, and as a gift from God, they are given to us as a responsibility—so we cannot say: I have the truth, but the truth came to us and impels us. We must learn to be moved and led by it. And then it will shine again: if the truth itself leads us and penetrates us.[58]

This is my auspicious wish for each one of us: that the search for the truth would reject every intellectual game incapable of penetrating and giving form to life, so that the light of the truth would always be above us and before us, and that, through an unmerited gift from above, it could conquer the force in the world also through us. Thank you!

From Latin America to the Universal Church

I. The Preferential Option for the Poor at Aparecida

Gustavo Gutierrez

As in the case of the preceding Conferences of the Episcopate of Latin America and of the Caribbean, that of Aparecida will mark the life of the Church on the Latin American continent and will have repercussions well beyond Aparecida.

The aforementioned conferences were part, and are the result, of long processes, in which a considerable part of the People of God participated. Following the road opened by the Second Vatican Council and, among these, starting with the Conference of Medellín, as well as in the sphere of the development of the conferences themselves, an active participation emerged of numerous and important lay people, priests, religious, and members of other Christian churches and of other religions. Such a contribution has been relevant also in the sphere of the Fifth Conference.[59]

The initial preparation of Aparecida goes back to the preceding years, with the involvement and fidelity of many to the Gospel and to the poor of this continent, despite all the difficulties and misunderstandings. As Aparecida itself recognizes, such preparation resides in "the courageous testimony of our men and women saints, and of those who, even though not canonized, have lived out the gospel radically, and have offered their life for Christ, for the Church, and for their people" (Aparecida [A]., no. 98).[60] Many of them are known, while others are anonymous, but all are "witnesses of the faith," as the document affirms (a recognition and a homage whose absence was felt in the preceding conferences). Hence why, in the eyes of all those who followed this line of thought from close up—one that is silent, but always alive—consisting in tasks and works in the life of the Church in Latin America, Aparecida is not a surprise.

The immediate course that led to this conference was marked out by dialogues and conversations with persons of diverse alliances, not to mention with numerous gatherings of CELAM in whose sphere the profile of the assembly was progressively defined. This openness was verified also during the days of the conference and contributed to its being transformed into an important moment in the life of the Church of Latin America and of the Caribbean. This climate surely will influence the period that follows, in which the reception of the event of Aparecida and its conclusions will play a decisive role.

The Marian sanctuary in which the Aparecida assembly occurred placed it in direct contact with the religiosity of a people whose interest and prayers have never been lacking in its regard. It is said that Aparecida signifies a ratification of the theological-pastoral line assumed in the last decades in the preceding continental encounters.[61] This is true for various reasons. At the same time, or rather precisely for this reason, with a glance turned again toward the time to come, this is done by taking into account the challenges which the desire to live and announce the gospel message must confront. It is good to give attention to this fidelity and openness if we want to understand the significance and weight of either this event or of the Aparecida document.

These pages do not pretend to be a commentary on the whole document,[62] but they do intend simply to deal with one of the pillars—a fundamental pillar, for sure, since it confers the structure on the entire text and offers us a substantial criterion for doing a reading of it—that is, the preferential option for the poor. In effect, as is affirmed in the final document, this perspective is "one of the distinguishing features of our Latin American and Caribbean Church" (A., no. 391). This approach is an expression of the maturity of a Church that, from the second half of the last century, was engaged in looking into the face of the social and cultural reality of the continent in which she must bear witness and proclaim the Good

News, faithful to the commandment of Jesus to seek the Kingdom and justice of God (see Mt 6:33).[63]

We will observe, in the first place, the insistence on knowing how to discern the signs of the times, as St. John XXIII asked when convoking the Council. Later on, we will examine how Aparecida presents the foundation and implications of the option for the poor. Finally, we will highlight one of its most important consequences: the relationship between the proclamation of the Gospel and the transformation of history.

Discerning the Signs of the Times

In the process that led up to Aparecida, the necessity of assuming once again the method of "seeing, judging, and acting" was progressively affirmed. The reading of a believer (since this is what concerns us) of the historical reality was considered of crucial importance to sketch the profile of the evangelizing presence of the Latin American Christian community. Moreover, the conference was situated in the open perspective of the conciliar days (with the encyclicals of St. John XXIII, the Constitution *Gaudium et Spes*, and other texts) whose presence, at Medellín, Puebla and, in a lesser way, at Santo Domingo, is well known.

A Reading from the Perspective of a Believer

From the very beginning, Aparecida sought to accomplish a faithful reading of reality and to place it in relation to its central theme: "As disciples of Jesus Christ, we feel challenged to discern the 'signs of the times' in the light of the Holy Spirit, to place ourselves at the service of the Kingdom proclaimed by Jesus who came so that all might have life and 'and have it more abundantly' (Jn 10:10) (A., no. 33).

IN CONTINUITY

The discernment presupposes "an attitude of ongoing pastoral conversion, which entails listening attentively and discerning 'what the

Spirit says to the churches' (Rev 2:29)" (A., no. 366). As we know well, in other times, St. John XXIII wanted to engage the topic. He did this in the text convoking the Second Vatican Council, *Humanae Salutis* (1960), being inspired by Matthew 16:3 and the prophetic books that contain what we could call a pedagogy of the discernment of the signs of the times (see, for example, Jer 1:11-19). Such pedagogy translates into a demanding apprenticeship, according to which a glance toward the historic future must be continually refined. The pope recalled this approach also in two great encyclicals: *Mater et Magistra* (1961) and *Pacem in Terris* (1963). It was, therefore, an appeal "to look to the distance," as the same St. John XXIII loved to repeat.

In the encyclical *Ecclesiam Suam*, of great influence at the Second Vatican Council, Pope Paul VI wished to return openly to the theme. Finally, we have conciliar documents and, at the beginning of *Gaudium et Spes*, in a well-known passage, highlighted is the need for the relationship between the Church and the world to scrutinize the signs of the times and to "interpret them in the light of the Gospel. Thus, in language intelligible to each generation, she can respond to the perennial questions which men ask about this present life and the life to come, and about the relationship of the one to the other" (no. 4).[64]

This general effect—concentrated on taking positions (also located at the elevated level of the Magisterium) in the conciliar years—made it so that this point of view would become one of the most important foundation stones of the Second Vatican Council. Among these positions, those which we discover in the Conferences of the Latin American Episcopate, beginning with Medellín, adopt such a perspective as the methodological axis of these texts. The repercussions in the life of the Christian community have been immense, and still are: they have opened the way to Christian involvement.

A PERMANENT ENGAGEMENT

The reception of the proposal of St. John XXII demonstrates its consonance with the Christian message and the believer's sensibility. It deals with a pivotal view of the Incarnation of the Son of God, who reveals the love of God for the human race in the process of its historic development. This is its theological foundation. Discerning what in human history corresponds to the demands and presence of the Kingdom from what, instead, reveals its absence is the task of the Church as a whole.[65] Effectively, in this journey, it appears clear from the beginning that the historical events to scrutinize are not only positive, but that there are also, of course, those that are not situated in line with gospel values. This intention to understand history is crucial for the task of proclaiming the Gospel, and it is in this horizon that the documents of St. John XXIII and the Council are situated. We find ourselves before a permanent work, one which must be renewed continually, as Aparecida affirmed. A series of events that have occurred in recent years—whether of an economic order, or one that is political and cultural, but also religious and Christian in particular—are producing at a dizzying rhythm an unheard of situation that makes many of our certainties and many historical endeavors waver. This concerns, without a doubt, a long process but it is also true that history, in recent times, has accelerated its pace.

Certainly, the modalities, with which the poor and the oppressed have entered into the historical scenario, are today completely different with respect to the past: one could say that they have, in fact, "entered into crisis" and have gone backward. Despite that, it is necessary to pay attention to the unheard of ways that are entered upon today. They express, with greater clarity with respect to preceding periods, the different dimensions of the condition of insignificance and discrimination. One cannot reduce what we have called "the irruption of the poor" to only one of its historical manifestations.

In this way, the sketch of the complex reality of the poor is completed progressively, by means of attempts and errors, in a way that is more or less strident, but which ends in becoming more precise and which summons us, so much so that Aparecida takes note of it. In other words, we find ourselves before a process *in itinere*, which is not yet totally fulfilled.

The Question of Method at Aparecida

The way to be followed to make precise the tasks of the Christian community nowadays in Latin America and in the Caribbean has been a theme tackled not only during the preparation of Aparecida, but also within the context of the Conference itself.

SEEING, JUDGING, AND ACTING

As we have recalled, using the analysis and interpretation of the social and historical reality as a point of departure has been a decisive element in the documents of Medellín and Puebla. This was not so at Santo Domingo, due to guidelines linked to a fear that beginning in this way would have given place, as was being asserted, to a certain "sociologism" that would have caused the loss, or at least would have heavily obstructed, the adoption of the perspective of the Christian faith.

This meant ignoring the sense of such a methodology that maintains, justly, that "seeing" is already a reading by a believer: those who apply this reading—from when Catholic Youth Action was launched and, later on, by Cardinal Cardijn himself—know this perfectly well. At Santo Domingo, some commissions sought to maintain this approach, but the general disposition that counseled against it had allowed for, despite some successes, an impoverishment of the final result. There was a great awareness at Aparecida with respect to all of this.

We wanted to remember this aspect, since it explains, in large measure, the insistence of the majority of the episcopates about the necessity of recuperating a methodology that allows for the reading of the signs of the times. The Document of Participation does not mention it, as one would have hoped. The Document of Synthesis instead speaks of it, in the contributions of the different Episcopal Conferences of the Latin American Continent, in which it is recognized that this method had been used, with profit, in the preceding Latin American Conferences (see nos. 34-36). The first schemata of the Final Document—that remained only on the level of a sketch—do not make mention of it, like the first two redactions of the same document, although they are partially aware of it. It was only thanks to a subsequent insistence that the Conference decided to adopt the theme explicitly, ratifying it and recognizing it through a vote that had the support of a large majority. All this is seen clearly from the summary of the document,[66] not to mention from the Final Document itself (see: A., no. 19, the number that remained from the third redaction).[67] In fact, after a chapter on missionary disciples, the concluding text is ordered on the basis of these three stages.

THE THEOLOGICAL PLACES

The discernment of the signs of the times and the method of "seeing, judging, and acting" reconnect themselves to the classic themes of *loci theologici*. This is a decisive contribution for a theological methodology that comes from Melchior Cano, a theologian of the School of Salamanca.

The new evaluation of the human history of the seventeenth century is not extraneous to this theme.[68] Cano seeks to be aware of this fact and proposes in a systematic way, although with a certain rigidity, what he calls "theological places": he sees them as fonts that furnish the material for theological reflection. Cano lists ten places, but does not put them all on the same level: Scripture and Tradition are those fundamental theological places that constitute the point of departure; among the eight remaining theological places, there are the life of the Church and her Magisterium, as well as theology, philosophical thought, and human history. In our opinion, maintaining the characteristic of the font nourishes the current tendency of considering that the theological place is also an ecclesial and social place, starting from which the discourse on the faith is elaborated.[69] The element that is the basis of this function, comprising the shades of meaning like those above, is the biblical fact of the presence of God in history.

The "Law of the Incarnation"

Marie-Dominique Chenu[70] uses the expression "the law of the Incarnation" as a hermeneutical key—whose source is the Incarnation of the Word of the Father of history—to comprehend the Christian message and the historical becoming of humanity.

The discourse of Pope Benedict XVI, of decisive importance for the conclusions of Aparecida,[71] insists on the God with a human face and, consequently, on his presence in history: "God is the foundational reality, not a God who is merely imagined or hypothetical, but God with a human face; he is God-with-us, the God who loves even to the Cross" (*Discourse*, no. 3). The Matthean theme of Emmanuel, of Old Testament origin, pervades his words and offers a solid help for speaking of the tasks that Christians, and the Church as a whole, must assume before the situation of Latin America and of the Caribbean.

At the beginning of his discourse, with a language that, in the past, some regarded with suspicion, the pope affirms that "the Word of God, in becoming flesh in Jesus Christ, also became history and culture" (*Discourse*, no. 1).[72] By becoming man, he enters into human history and is situated in a culture. This involves necessary dimensions full of consequences for an appropriate comprehension of the Christian message: a message that is fulfilled in history and that, at the same time, transcends it.

THE REAFFIRMATION OF THE PREFERENTIAL OPTION FOR THE POOR

The link between God and the poor pervades the entire Bible. Bartolomé de las Casas manifests it in a beautiful and expressive thought that becomes for him a model of conduct for solidarity with and the defense of the native inhabitants of those lands. Worth noting is what he says about them, speaking of a continental ecclesial assembly: "From the smallest and the most forgotten, God keeps the most living and recent memory." This memory is present in Aparecida and on it is based the preferential option for the poor, a contemporary expression of an always crucial element of the Christian message.

We assume "this option for the poor with new energy" (A., no. 399); "our option is confirmed . . ." (*Summary*, no. 6); "we re-affirm our option" (*Message*, no. 4); we maintain "with renewed energy our option" (ibid.). The texts of Aparecida multiply these statements: with these, clearly manifested is the will to be located in a strengthened and creative continuity with the preferential option for the poor, a perspective adopted by the Church of Latin America and of the Caribbean in the last decades. This option, as an already-mentioned text says, traces a profile of "one of the distinguishing features" of the Church on the Continent (A., no. 391). It is a conviction that Aparecida puts forward as a point of no return for the Church that lives on this Continent.[73]

1. The Christological Foundation

Undoubtedly, one of the most relevant assertions of the inaugural discourse of Pope Benedict XVI, which had a great influence on the final text, concerns the theological foundation of the option for the poor. Confronting this theme, and doing so in extremely clear terms, before the Episcopal Conference of the Latin American Continent where the formulation of this solidarity with the poor was born, was particularly significant.

The pope frames this option by recalling that the Christian faith makes us move out of individualism and creates communion with God and, consequently, among ourselves: "Faith releases us from the isolation of the 'I,' because it leads us to communion: the encounter with God is, in itself and as such, an encounter with our brothers and sisters, an act of convocation, of unification, of responsibility toward the other and toward others." The option for the poor is a way toward communion and finds in itself its most profound and demanding significance. The text just cited continues, immediately after, as follows: "In this sense, the preferential option for the poor is implicit in the Christological faith in the God who became poor for us, so as to enrich us with his poverty (cf. 2 Cor

8:9)" (*Discourse*, no. 3). It is the faith in a God who became one with us and who manifests himself in the witness of the special love that Jesus Christ has for the poor.

It is on this paradigm of the Incarnation that the text appears cited at Aparecida. "Our faith proclaims that"—it affirms, basing itself on a phrase from the exhortation *Ecclesia in America* (no. 67)—"Jesus Christ [is] the human face of God and the divine face of man." Then the citation from the discourse of the pope continues: "For this reason, 'the preferential option for the poor is implicit in the Christological faith in the God who became poor for us, so as to enrich us with his poverty (*Discourse*, no. 3).'" The "for this reason," which equals the "in this sense" of the papal discourse, as well as the mention of the face, human and divine, of Christ, reaffirm at the same time the foundation of this option: faith in Christ. Here is the root of everything. This is what Aparecida maintains very clearly: "This option arises out of our faith in Jesus Christ, God made man, who has become our brother (cf. Heb 2:11-12) " (A., no. 392).[74] The brotherhood between Christ and human beings, the communion of which the inaugural discourse speaks, is accentuated at Aparecida with the reference to the Letter to the Hebrews.

Two numbers later, taken up again is the idea of the option for the poor as implicit in Christological faith or as flowing from it: "Solidarity likewise springs from our faith in Christ as a permanent attitude of encounter, brotherly and sisterly spirit, and service" (A., no. 394). These different terms underscore the relationship between Christ and the option for the poor. Such a link is recalled also in the theological reflection which accompanied these considerations and which we find in the three preceding Latin American conferences. In them the Christological foundation of the option for the poor appears clearly.[75] Moreover, all the Conferences make reference to the same text of 2 Corinthians 8:9, to which both Pope Benedict XVI and Aparecida allude. Undoubtedly, however, the formulation that we find in their texts confers precision, currency, and great vigor on a perspective that put an indelible mark on the life of the Church on the Continent and also beyond it. In this way, the option for the poor is set up as a pillar of the document of

Aparecida, which it truly is, precisely because it deals with a pillar of life and reflection for the disciple of Jesus.[76]

2. The Faces of the Poor

The document draws an important consequence from what was said about the foundation of the option for the poor: "If this option is implicit in Christological faith, we Christians as disciples and missionaries are called to contemplate, in the suffering faces of our brothers and sisters, the face of Christ who calls us to serve him in them." The document re-connects with a text from Santo Domingo: "The suffering faces of the poor are suffering faces of Christ" (A., no. 393). This recognition implies "see[ing] with the eyes of faith" (A., no. 32).

This topic, of evident evangelical inspiration, emerged, as we know, at Puebla (nos. 31-39). Its reception in the Christian communities of the Continent and in many of its liturgical celebrations was enormous. Santo Domingo reprised it, amplifying the list of these and asked that it subsequently be enriched. This is what Aparecida did, taking up again this idea of the Latin American ecclesial tradition of the last decades. But there is more: in Aparecida we have two lists of the new faces of the poor in which we must recognize that of Christ.[77]

Sustained, with precision and firmness, is that the challenge that comes from these suffering faces penetrates things in great depth: "They question the core of the Church's action, its ministry, and our Christian attitudes" (A., no. 393). The reason is clear and demanding, since "Whatever you did for one of these least brothers of mine, you did for me" (Mt 25:40). Therefore, there is a strict relationship between Christ and the poor. The crucial text of Matthew 25, extremely present in the history of the evangelization of and solidarity with the poor of this Continent, is the foundation of this perspective. This is why it is the biblical passage most studied in the sphere of liberation theology.[78]

In the matter at hand, the number of Aparecida that we are citing ends with a new Christological reference: "John Paul II emphasized that this biblical text 'sheds a ray of light on the mystery of Christ.'[79] For in Christ the great became small, the strong became weak, the rich became poor" (A., no. 393). In fact, the text of Matthew is not limited to a pure question of comportment on the part of the Christian, to a fact of an ethic of evangelical inspiration: rather, it indicates to us a way to follow in order to understand Emmanuel, the God-with-us, the God present in human history. If we do not push ourselves to this point, we will not be able to understand the depth and full import of it. The contrasts presented by the cited phrase are particularly significant and evocative.

The concluding text of the first chapter of Aparecida reassumes perfectly what is in this paragraph: "In the face of Jesus Christ, dead and risen, bruised for our sins and glorified by the Father, in this suffering and glorious face,[80] we can see with the eyes of faith the humiliated face of so many men and women of our peoples, and at the same time, their calling to the freedom of the children of God, to the full realization of their personal dignity and to brotherhood among all. The Church is at the service of all human beings, sons and daughters of God" (A., no. 32).

3. The Preference for the Poor

This is an option that implies a decided solidarity and involvement. The poor are the first in the love of God for everyone; the preference does not weaken the demand of this option; it is with a preferential option, as is oftentimes reiterated. Both terms, option and preference, are utilized and deepened in the Aparecida document.

4. A Kairos: The Emergence of the Poor

What has been identified as "the 'irruption' of the poor in the life of the Continent," has brought with it a reflection on this sign of the times, in the light of faith.

This way has brought about a biblical study, which results in a proposal of the option for the poor. However, the solidarity that it implies refers to the real poor, to those who live in a situation of injustice and social insignificance, contrary to the will of the God of love. The document adopts this approach and, starting with the situation of the poor and the marginalized in our days, takes up again with strength some points on which lived experience and reflection on the option for the poor in these years have insisted.

In the first place, the Document delineates a perception of the complexity of poverty, which is not limited to its economic dimension, although that dimension remains very important. It affirms: "the scourge of poverty . . . has different expressions: economic, physical, spiritual, moral, and so forth" (A., no. 176). From here is derived its sensibility in relation to the "cultural diversity" of the Continent, that it considers "obvious" (A., no. 56).[81] The text values and takes into consideration a "*kairos*," a propitious moment in the new presence of indigenous and African descendants that can also lead us to "a new Pentecost."[82] In a good formulation, the conclusions maintain that "the indigenous and Afro-Americans are particularly different 'others,' who demand respect and recognition. Society tends to look down on them, ignoring their uniqueness" (A., no. 89).[83] In fact, the poor person is "the other" within a society that does not recognize, at least no more than theoretically, his human dignity.

On this same pathway, and accentuating the complexity of the world of marginalization and social insignificance, Aparecida confronts the question of the situation of women: "At this time in Latin America and the Caribbean, there must be greater awareness of the difficult situation affecting the dignity of many women" (A., no. 48; see also nos. 451-458), who suffer a terrible exclusion for various reasons: "Many women . . . are excluded because of their sex, race, or socioeconomic situation" (A., no. 65).[84] Also important for them is the question of the type of "otherness" mentioned since, in a certain way, the woman is "another" with respect to the present society: she is a person whose proper human dignity and rights are not fully recognized.

There is, then, another relevant aspect in this text that puts an accent on women who belong to particularly marginalized populations, while underscoring the actuality and care that need to be exercised in this state of things. It affirms: "At this time in Latin

America and the Caribbean, the so often silenced cry of women who are subjected to many forms of exclusion and violence in all their forms and at all stages of their lives must be heard. Among them, poor, indigenous and Afro-American women have endured double marginalization" (A., no. 454). The Puebla text of "Preferential Option for the Poor" already warns us against this double marginalization. Much still remains to be said about the new faces of poverty and about the new spheres that suffer strong exclusion and social and cultural insignificance. Nevertheless, in this matter, as in many others, Aparecida does not intend to close either the analysis or the reflection.

The document also highlights the *causes* of various types of poverty.[85] Let us limit ourselves to mentioning what it says about globalization, a topic present at various points in the Aparecida text. Let us begin with an affirmation of the totality: "Globalization is causing the emergence of new faces of the poor in our peoples" (A., no. 402). The reason is found in the fact that "in globalization, market forces easily absolutize efficacy and productivity as values regulating all human relations. This peculiar character makes globalization a process that fosters many inequities and injustices" (A., no. 61). This is due to the tendency for globalization to favor and "prize profit and stimulate competition . . . augmenting the inequalities that sadly characterize our continent and that keep large numbers of people in poverty" (A., no. 62). Let us specify that, in every instance, the conclusions make perfectly clear that they refer to globalization "in its current form" (A., no. 61), since it could adopt other courses.

Aparecida gives attention to a cardinal point of Latin American practice and reflection about the option for the poor: the poor themselves must be able *to control their own destiny*. This does not have to do with speaking for the poor: what is important is that the poor themselves have a voice in a society that does not listen to their cry for liberation and justice. This is their most profound aspiration; they feel "the need to shape [their] own destiny" (A., no. 53). In this regard, the process of the "recovery of identity" of the marginalized peoples is affirmed, "enabling black women and men to be architects of their own history, a new history that is taking shape in Latin America and the Caribbean today" (A., no. 97). The same principle goes for other weak elements and those in different fields: "Day by day the poor become agents of evangelization and of comprehensive human promotion" (A., no. 398).

5. Preference

In the 1960s and in particular at Medellín, the bases were laid for what, in the preceding years at Puebla, had begun to be called a prioritized action on behalf of the poor: action that is "preferential," "privileged," or similar expressions. In fact, the three key words of the phrase "preferential option for the poor," correspond, one by one, to the three accepted meanings of the term "poverty" according to the distinction embraced by Medellín: real poverty as an unjust and inhumane condition; spiritual poverty and solidarity with the poor; and the rejection of poverty.[86]

The term "preference" does not mean to moderate—and even less to forget—the demand for solidarity with the poor and with social justice. It cannot be understood, except in relation to the love of God for every person. Scripture presents it as universal and, at the same time, preferential. It is to this that St. John XXIII was referring when he spoke of "a Church of all and *particularly* of the poor." Here are two aspects that are not really in contradiction but in a fruitful tension. Limiting oneself to one of them means losing both.

For this reason, Aparecida says—at the beginning of Chapter 8, which deals in particular with the option for the poor—that "the mission of proclaiming the good news of Jesus Christ has a universal destination. Its mandate of charity encompasses all dimensions of existence, all people, all environments of community life, and all peoples. Nothing human can be alien to it" (A., no. 380). It is in this context that the sense of the priority of marginalized and excluded persons is to be understood.

The document means just this when it speaks of the option for the poor and affirms that its being "preferential means that it should permeate all our pastoral structures and priorities. The Latin

American Church is called to be sacrament of love, solidarity, and justice within our peoples" (A., no. 396). It must be a bridge to all the ecclesial instances—and not pigeonholed in certain sectors—so that it might be a sacrament of love and justice. Preference tends to this goal, not to attenuate the radical nature of the option.

On the one hand, universality situates the privilege of the poor in a wide horizon, positioning them to overcome continually the possible limits; at the same time, the preference for the poor confers concreteness and historic importance on this universality, guarding against the danger of remaining anchored at a deceptive and obscure level.

Evangelization and Engagement for Justice

Various questions derive from the way in which the preferential option for the poor is affirmed and presented at Aparecida. In this lecture, we will limit ourselves to taking note of one of them in particular.

Following what we have said, what in its own turn is the result of decades of a trajectory in which vicissitudes have not been lacking, the document expresses a wide and fruitful vision of evangelization. Very early in the text, it affirms that missionary disciples[87] know that the light of Christ guarantees hope, love, and the future, and it adds: "This is the essential task of evangelization, which includes the preferential option for the poor, integral human promotion, and authentic Christian liberation" (A., no. 146). In fact, one of the implications of this option concerns the witness of the Good News.

I. Sharing an Experience

The proclamation of the Gospel comes from an encounter: namely, from an encounter with Jesus. We have found the Messiah, the Christ, says Andrew to his brother, Simon Peter, as he leads him to Jesus (see Jn 1:41-42). This is a simple account that tells us in what the fulcrum of the communication of the Good News consists. To remember this, let us allow the document to express considerations that are near to us, that are part of many experiences, and that are part of the very meaning of the option for the poor.

The Joy of the Disciple

This sharing is born from the joy of the "the encounter with Jesus Christ, whom we recognize as Son of God incarnate and redeemer . . . [and] we want the good news of the Kingdom of God, of Jesus Christ victorious over sin and death, to reach all . . . and making him known by our word and deeds is our joy" (A., no. 29). Without this experience, the transmission of the message becomes something cold and distant that does not reach people. The option for the poor, in fact, does not avoid the risk of "remaining on a theoretical or merely emotional level, without truly impacting our behavior and our decisions" (A., no. 397). The joyful experience of the encounter with Jesus amplifies our views and opens our hearts.

The option for the poor asks us to "to devote time to the poor, provide them kind attention, listen to them with interest, stand by them in the most difficult moments, choosing to spend hours, weeks, or years of our life with them, and striving to transform their situation" (ibid.). This is not a question of condescension, but rather of solidarity and friendship. Friendship signifies equality, and recognition of their dignity. The document intends it precisely thus, which is why it reiterates that it is necessary to avoid "any paternalistic attitude" (ibid.).

Hidden Poverties

"Only the closeness that makes us friends," says Aparecida, "enables us to appreciate deeply the values of the poor today, their legitimate desires, and their own manner of living the faith. The option for the poor should lead us to friendship with the poor" (A., no. 398).[88] Without friendship with them, in fact, there is no authentic solidarity nor true sharing; the option is one for concrete persons, for daughters and sons of God.

This attitude will help us to perceive "the great suffering endured by most of our people often in the form of hidden poverties" (A., no. 176), affirms Aparecida with sensitivity and insight. There are humble poverties among the poor: barely visible, made from daily life, so assimilated that one doesn't even speak of them. These impositions are seen as inevitable facts, and the poor have a certain shame that covers these poverties with a veil of silence. This happens above all with women from the poorest sectors who are marginalized, often in the very sphere of their own families, but this does not happen only with them. All these little (or great) sufferings come to the surface—when they make it—only after a long period of friendship, and often we excuse ourselves from even speaking about them. It is precisely to that point that one needs to push forward.

These considerations do not exclude, in any way, that the option for the poor would signify, equally, an engagement for justice and a solidarity equipped with the necessary attempts to eliminate it, as we will see in the next paragraph. These are listed here simply to highlight some crucial aspects which do not delve deeply enough into the profound—and humble—dimensions of the life of the poor, not to mention the more delicate aspects of human beings.

II. The Church, Advocate of Justice and of the Poor

The option for the poor is included in the task of evangelization, as Pope Benedict XVI said, in a phrase that we cited just a short while ago. This brings us to ask ourselves about the place of the struggle for justice within the proclamation of the Kingdom.

A Prophetic Word

Action for justice and human promotion are not extraneous to evangelization. On the contrary, they do not end where the proclamation of the Christian message begins; this is not a pre-evangelization, but constitutes a part of the proclamation of the Good News. This vision, today ever more evident—and as it is likewise in Aparecida—is the result of a process that little by little has made us understand the meaning of the expression, "thy Kingdom come." It means speaking of the transformation of history in which the Kingdom of God is rendered *already* present, although *not yet* fully so. This is a movement that picks up speed, beginning with the Council, when the Church in the world was seriously considered.

In this regard, Medellín affirms that Jesus came to free us from sin, whose consequences are a slavery that is summed up in injustice (*Justice*, no. 3); the point was reprised later, in one way or another, by the subsequent continental assemblies. The Roman Synod on

Justice in the World (1971) follows this line: the mission of the Church "involves defending and promoting the dignity and fundamental rights of the human person" (no. 37). Besides *Evangelii Nuntiandi* (no. 29), St. John Paul II expresses the exact same concept at Puebla, almost with the same terms of the Synod, mentioning that the Church's "evangelizing mission has, as an essential part, action for justice and the tasks of the advancement of man" (*Discourse*, III, no. 2).

For his part, in the inaugural discourse, Pope Benedict XVI affirmed that "evangelization has always developed alongside the promotion of the human person and authentic Christian liberation" (*Discourse,* no. 3) and that "love of God and love of neighbor have become one: in the least of the brethren we find Jesus himself, and in Jesus we find God" (*Deus Caritas Est*, no. 15). This is a question of principle, which historical infidelities to this claim do not modify since it is a permanent exigency.[89] In this order of ideas, Pope Benedict XVI declares openly, in a text very influential for Aparecida, that "the Church is the advocate of justice and of the poor" and some lines later, he reiterates the idea: the Church is "advocate of justice and truth" (*Discourse*, no. 4). These texts are often cited at Aparecida and are filled out with concepts that deepen their significance. "The Holy Father has reminded us that the Church is called to be 'advocate of justice and of the poor' in the face of intolerable social and economic inequalities" (A., no. 395). The point is clear. The proclamation of the Gospel is a prophetic word that proclaims the love of God for every person, but principally for the poor and neglected: a prophetic word that denounces the situation of the injustice they suffer.

The proclamation of the Gospel implies a transformation of history which revolves around justice, a respectful evaluation of class distinctions, ethnic and cultural, and the defense of the most elementary human rights, on which a society founded on equality and fraternity must be based: a society of "more human" conditions as *Populorum Progressio* maintains (no. 21), cited by Pope Benedict XVI in his inaugural discourse.

The Table of Life

Denouncing injustices and re-establishing justice are necessary expressions of solidarity in relation to concrete persons.[90] We believe in a God of life, who condemns the inhumane poverty which is nothing more than unjust and premature death. All of us are called to participate in the banquet of life, as the Conference affirms: "The acute differences between rich and poor invite us to work with greater effort in being disciples who know how to share the table of life, the table of all the sons and daughters of the Father, an open table, inclusive, in which no one is left behind. Therefore, we reinforce our preferential and evangelical option for the poor" (*Final Message*, no. 4). An open table, therefore, from which no one is excluded; however, the first of those invited are the last of this world.

The Holy Father, in his inaugural discourse, wanted to make an interesting allusion to the danger of the contemporary world: that of an individualistic and indifferent attitude in relation to the reality in which we live. Aparecida picks up this observation in the same terms: "Holiness is not a flight toward self-absorption or toward religious individualism," a very marked tendency in society and in today's religious world. The Discourse insists that holiness does not mean "abandoning the urgent reality of the enormous economic, social, and political problems of Latin America and the world, let alone a flight from reality toward an exclusively spiritual world" (*Discourse*, no. 3, text cited in A., no. 148). This, in fact, is a great contemporary temptation of the Christian life, to which many yield and of which they even boast; this temptation permits one to feel at peace with one's conscience even if he abandons the witness of Jesus. As if a self-absorbed and isolated attitude, pretending to move into an "exclusively spiritual" sphere, could respond faithfully to the demands of the Gospel. In this sense, the pope and Aparecida launch a great warning in the face of this "purism," which does not correspond to the authentic purity and clarity of the Gospel.[91]

The ecclesial base communities "deploy their evangelizing and missionary commitment among the humblest and most distant, and they visibly express the preferential option for the poor" (A., no. 179),[92] highlighting precisely the solidarity that is born from love of God and love of neighbor, both of which are a part of a "single commandment" (*Deus Caritas Est*, no. 18). In the Eucharist, configuring ourselves to the Lord and listening to his Word in prayer, we make a memorial of his life, witness, teaching, Death, and Resurrection, and we celebrate with joy our communion with God and with one other (see A., no. 142).

Conclusion

The document is marked with hope, but it is not made up of illusions. Toward the end of the text, it makes clear that "there is certainly no other region" like that of Latin America and the Caribbean. However, there is "a unity torn apart because it is permeated by deep dominations and contradictions, still incapable of bringing together into itself 'all the races' and overcoming the gap of tremendous inequality and marginalization" (A., no. 527). The expression, "*todas las sangres*," comes from the title of a novel by José Maria Arguedas, in which the author seeks to describe the complex reality of Peru, but which in reality is valid for the entire Continent. It expresses our diversity, but also our richness and our potentialities: to indicate the difficulties that we must confront in the present is the question of realism, and it is an indispensable condition for correctly meeting head-on the challenges that arise from our situation.

Aparecida has sought to look this reality directly in the face, without subterfuges or shortcuts. It raises questions for the disciples of Jesus Christ, so that they might fulfill their mission in fidelity to the Gospel. It does this, convinced that "the preferential option for the poor impels us as disciples and missionaries of Jesus to seek new and creative paths in order to respond to other effects of poverty" (A., no. 409), but also in its causes and in a multitude of additional consequences. This option encompasses a style of life that has inspired many forms of engagement at three levels, different among themselves although linked: the proclamation of the Good News (in the pastoral and social field), perhaps the most visible; that of the theological; and, as the foundation of what I have just said, that of spirituality, the *sequela Christi*. This is what makes it one of the essential pillars of the document.

At the beginning of these pages, we said that the event and the document of Aparecida will mark the life of the Church of Latin America and of the Caribbean for years to come, but it is necessary to complete this affirmation. Everything depends on how we will receive Aparecida: it is in our hands,[93] in the hands of the local churches, of the Christian communities, and of the diverse ecclesial applications. Exegesis—the interpretation of texts like this—is fulfilled in facts, in practice. It is to this that the Good News of the Kingdom of God calls us here and now.

I. The Spirituality of the Conciliar Event[94]
Gustavo Gutierrez

Fifty some years ago, the Council—which, to the surprise of many, was convoked by St. John XXIII—was about to begin a second session, after a rocky beginning in 1962. In the first session, in fact, some were thinking—and hoping—that the Council would last only a few months and would approve, with little discussion and some touch-up, the schemata of the documents prepared by the Roman Curia. This did not happen. During this first phase, in fact, all the schemata that had been previously prepared were rejected— except for one, that on the liturgy—but the initial debates allowed the participants to get to know one another and to create a climate of dialogue and openness that would mark the endeavors thenceforth. During the last days of the first session, a course to follow was designed and the Council reconvened, opening a new stage in the life of the Catholic Church.

As we know, the Council concluded in an atmosphere of great joy for those who had participated in its endeavors, for those who had been able to follow them from close up, and also for world public opinion, surprised by the warmth and humanistic openness of its message. Its documents were—and still are—redacted with evangelical inspiration, starting from the notion that one dialogs with today's world in a framework of a proposal of service. Despite this, in the same conciliar years, there were some disagreements and resistances which, although minor, presaged that, in some circles, there would be a persistent critical position with regard to the posture assumed by the Second Vatican Council: a posture that, later on, would assume various forms. An initial correction, and one that still recurs, was that of the so-called reduction of the Christian message to a level that is simply human, one that puts aside spiritual and religious dimensions. The decades which followed the ecclesial event of major importance in the last centuries of the history of the People of God were characterized by lights and shadows.[95]

In the memorable discourse at the closing of the Council (December 7, 1965), still very relevant, Pope Paul VI, anticipating what could take place, decided to take the bull by the horns. His words underscored what he called "the religious value of this Council," defending the positive and humanistic character of the presentation of the Christian message, which does not separate the inseparable: love of God and love of one's neighbor. He makes this precise: "The old story of the Samaritan has been the model of the spirituality of the council. A feeling of boundless sympathy has permeated the whole of it. The attention of our council has been absorbed by the discovery of human needs" (no. 8). This is the profound and expressive text that will be the main theme of these pages.

In our investigation, we will establish a relationship between the text of Pope Paul VI and its reference to the Gospel of Luke, and what we will be able to consider as the conciliar event. In the matter at hand, I am alluding to the whole reality made up of three elements: (a) the witness and voice of St. John XXIII during the preparation of the Council, to the extent that some intuitions were presented that were then re-elaborated by the Council, and others that were not deepened in its conclusions;[96] at the center of everything, one finds, of course: (b) the constitutions and decrees elaborated and approved by the Council that deepen and actualize the meaning of the message of Christ, expressed through "words and works" (*Dei Verbum*, no. 4) and refresh the ways of communicating it; (c) from the point of view of Latin America and of the Caribbean, the Episcopal Conference that took place in Medellín (Colombia) in 1968, only three years after the Council, was also part of the conciliar event, in a certain sense. This conference, which had as its theme "The Church in the Present Transformation of Latin

America in Light of the Council," was the first and, in many ways, the only continental reception of the conciliar message, which pervaded its conclusions with evident repercussions on various sectors of the universal Church, particularly in the poor countries. This reception was, for the most part, an example of creative fidelity.

In the Footsteps of Jesus

At the beginning of his discourse, Pope Paul VI cites a text of his predecessor—whom he calls "the author of the synod"—which, in his opinion, sets the objective of the Council: "The Lord has said: 'Seek first the kingdom of God and His justice.' The word 'first' expresses the direction in which our thoughts and energies must move" (*Discourse*, no. 3). This search is the heart of what we call spirituality.

What is meant when speaking of the spirituality of the Council? The word spirituality captures the sense of the traditional expression *sequela Christi*; it is a step forward which feeds off the memory of the witness of Jesus; its purpose and significance flow from the search for the Kingdom and justice of God. Memory, which, as Augustine affirms, is "the present of the past," is called a permanent reality. Currently, we use the term spirituality to indicate the journey of every Christian following after Jesus. This significance, however, although authentic, does not say everything; it is important to complete its meaning by considering its communal character. Here we are dealing with the progress of a people, of a journey that we make together with others, in *ecclesia*, and that directs us toward the God of the Kingdom. In this sense, Pope Paul VI affirms that we must consider love toward the human being "not as a means but as the first step toward the final and transcendent goal" (*Discourse*, no. 17). Jesus announces to us that we will find God along our historical itinerary.

The way is a classic metaphor, with biblical roots, present in the history of spirituality, in particular in Christian mysticism. In the Gospel of John, Jesus says that he is "the way and the truth and the life" (Jn 14:6), an expression that, perhaps, gave rise to the use—which we do not find, or at the very least not in the same way, in other places of the New Testament—to which the Book of the Acts of the Apostles refers, in the most significant way, to the Christian community, the Church, that it calls nine times "the way." Most of the time, Acts uses the term without qualifications, in a very straightforward manner (see Acts 9:2; 19:9, 23; 22:4; 24:14, 22); on other occasions, however, the sacred author is more precise: "a way of salvation" (16:17), "the Way of the Lord" (18:25), "the Way of God" (18:26).[97] The metaphor of the way permits us to speak of passages completed according to a certain sustained rhythm and with accelerations; but also of slowness and obstacles, of eventual deviations, and of attempts to rediscover the road. John of the Cross knew this well, when he mentioned (and designated!) different pathways that lead us to the summit of Mount Carmel. There is also need for time here; it is a movement forward that crosses different moments of the life of persons and peoples who are continually renewed. For a variety of reasons, the initial presence of this word used to recall the ecclesial community manifests a rich intuition that we must not lose.

The Church is the People of God, "the messianic people" (*Lumen Gentium*, no. 9) who journeys along the course of history. On this path, hours of uncertainty and solitude are not lacking. When this spiritual process is lived within a marginalized people—as occurs in Latin America and in the Caribbean—the suffering of the innocent grabs our attention; one observes two resistances on the part of the active powers of our societies; one lives perplexities full of suffering on account of the distance and sometimes the misunderstandings of important ecclesiastical sectors, and what emerges, at times, is the sorrowful sentiment due to the perception of a God absent from our lives. They are situations in which, following the path of Jeremiah, we are tempted to say to God: "To me you are like a deceptive brook, waters that cannot be relied on!" (Jer 15:18). With the author of Lamentations, at the end, however, we will say: "Remembering it over and over, my soul is downcast. But this I will call to mind; therefore I will hope: The Lord's acts of mercy are not exhausted, his compassion is not spent" (Lam 3:20-22). And we continue our journey.

It is thus that one needs to understand the spirituality to which the Council opens us: it reminds us that the Church, inasmuch as it is a people, lives in history, journeying and taking out "the new and the old" (Mt 13:52). This is precisely what the conciliar assembly accomplished with lucidity and courage. New things and old things, in this order, let us not forget. How can we say today, St. John XXIII asked, "thy Kingdom come"? A rigid vision of the Christian message fears the openness and the response, always new, which the Gospel presents to the situations that are born progressively in the course of history. It denies the genius and dynamism of the sources which feed a true and proper continuity and which keep the message and witness of Jesus young. The Second Vatican Council, without hesitation, situates the Church before the modern world that rose up in the last centuries.

Since the task of the Church consists in continuing the mission of Christ, who came to serve and not to be served, through the evolution and vicissitudes of history, it is necessary to pay attention to what the Lord tells us through its becoming. For this reason, St. John XXIII wanted to recover a perspective of a biblical kind to make a lasting imprint on spirituality and on the reflection of many Christians for years to come. I am referring to the discernment of the signs of the times. The Holy Father wanted to recall it, and the Council welcomed his words. He said that we must "make our own Jesus' recommendation that we learn to discern 'the signs of the times' (Mt 16:3)" and, alluding to the Council, he added, "in the midst of so much darkness, more than a few indications that enable us to have hope for the fate of the Church and of humanity."[98] It is the analysis of the signs of the times that Pope Paul VI takes up in the text on which we are commenting. This topic is part of the personal experience of St. John XXIII,[99] so much as to cause him to write in his *Journal of a Soul*: "It is not the Gospel that changes; it is we who begin to understand it better. . . . The moment has arrived when we must recognize the signs of the times, seize the opportunity, and look far ahead."[100]

This question becomes one of the cardinal points of the Council. *Gaudium et Spes* opens the panoramic vision of "the situation of men in the modern world," affirming that "the Church has always had the duty of scrutinizing the signs of the times and of interpreting them in the light of the Gospel. Thus, in language intelligible to each generation, she can respond to the perennial questions which men ask about this present life and the life to come, and about the relationship of the one to the other" (no. 4).[101]

The question of the signs of the times is, above all, a perspective, a way of dealing with the great problems that the evangelizing task of the Church must confront. It concerns a methodological question, but we use it in a desire to strip this term of the rigidity and formal aspects that sometimes are related to it, for the purpose of recuperating not only the meaning of the intellectual journey, but also of the spiritual path which inspired it. In this order of ideas, for the purpose of offering a true evangelical witness, St. John XXIII proposes to the conciliar assembly the carrying out of a discernment before three historical situations, three "signs of the times" that we could define as: the modern world, the world of ecumenical dialogue, and the world of poverty. The first two proposals were treated with lucidity and in an atmosphere of dialogue.[102] The third, however, despite the attempts of some bishops and theologians close to the vision of St. John XXIII—among whom, in particular, was Cardinal Lercaro—is only treated in the final documents of the Council; despite this, it was received by the Episcopal Conference of Medellín.

Therefore, St. John XXIII, Vatican II, and Medellín opened a path that many Christians, and the Church in its totality, has journeyed in these years, not without difficulties and misunderstandings, offering a witness that, in many cases, was characterized by the blood of martyrdom of those who were engaged with the poor and the marginalized of our society: a sorrowful confirmation of the fact that these pastoral and theological perspectives were not abstract questions.

The Old Story of the Samaritan

In the discourse already mentioned, Pope Paul VI presents charity as the fulcrum of the Council. He affirms that "no one can reprove as want of religion or infidelity to the Gospel such a basic orientation, when we recall that it is Christ Himself who taught us that love for our brothers is the distinctive mark of His disciples (cf. Jn 13:35)" (*Discourse*, no. 7).

The mention of the story of the Samaritan is revelatory (see Lk 10:29-37) since it indicates how to live the *sequela* of Jesus.[103] The gesture of the Samaritan must inspire the practice of charity among the disciples of Jesus. This account has strongly marked the Christian memory and has inspired many works of art. In it, the supremacy of the other and the necessity to abandon the road to encounter the other is highlighted: one of the strong themes of Jesus' message. Although this is the attitude to have in relation to every person, it becomes even more demanding in the case of those who live in a situation of social marginalization; this is a text that is strictly linked to the meaning of the scene of the final judgment recounted in Matthew 25. It is to this same link that Pope Paul VI also alludes in his discourse.

The parable is told after a dialogue on the love of God and love of neighbor that moves a doctor of the law to ask Jesus: "Who is *my* neighbor?" The response that he receives is not a conceptual definition, but rather a motivational account: that of a person injured by human hand and, of the three characters, of whom only one draws near to help him; in the end, Jesus does nothing more than turn the initial question around, with a movement that offers the key to the meaning of the parable: "Who of these three seems to you *to have been a neighbor* to the one who fell into the hands of robbers?" The wise man responds by recognizing that it was the Samaritan: that is, the one who drew near and helped the needy and maltreated man, thus *making himself* his neighbor, a neighbor of the other. We are invited to realize that the neighbor is not one who is near, but one to whom we draw near. Making one's neighbor become the other means drawing near to the injured person, something which the first two travelers did not do, but which only the Samaritan did because he was moved to abandon his way to take care of him.[104] The Gospel of Jesus consists, precisely, in the call to abandon the universe focused on the egocentric "I," in the true sense of the term, and in this way, to enter into the world of the other, the world of the "you." This is so for persons, but also for the Christian community; as Pope Francis says, it is necessary that "the Church constantly go out from herself, keeping her mission focused on Jesus Christ, and her commitment to the poor" (*Evangelii Gaudium*, no. 97).

The question of Jesus brings about an opening: the axis of the question is moved, and the one who stands on the side of the road becomes the center of the question. Now, the heart of the event is no longer the "I" of the one who asked ("*my* neighbor"), but is found in the "you" of the one who was mistreated and forgotten (becoming a neighbor to the injured). He is the one who defines the attitude of the three travelers (the priest, the Levite, and the Samaritan); the condition of the one who became the victim of robbery and mistreatment will define the meaning of "nearness." We pass from our world to that of the other, and this movement constitutes the nucleus of the parable. The first two travelers did not become a neighbor to the injured man, but the Samaritan did, creating solidarity with him. Nearness is not a simple physical or cultural nearness, but the result of a gesture, a choice. This opening, which is like a Copernican revolution, is the inversion of two worlds: that of the lawyer (of the "I") who yields his place to that of the injured person (the "*you*," the other). And this is particularly significant in a Gospel like that of Luke, attentive to the historic drastic changes brought about by the Messiah: manifestations of the so-called "messianic inversion."

Consequently, beyond appearances, speaking in terms of the narrative, the key character of the account is not the Samaritan, but the one whom the passage calls "a man" (Lk 10:30), that is, the victim, without any protection, without either a name or identity. It does not say anything about him; he is an anonymous and "insignificant" personage; we do not know if he belonged to the Hebrew people or to the Samaritan people; we do not know what may have been his occupation or what he did in those places. He is "the other" and he (this other) functions as one whom the other personages of the narration will define; his condition as a maltreated and abandoned man catches the attention of those who find themselves immersed in daily human affairs, as they move from one place to another.

All the other actors of the account, however, are described through their religious identity or their place in society; this is true also for the innkeeper and even for the robbers . . . The anonymity and social nakedness of the victim manifest his insignificance; he remains only an appearance to them. His humanity, his countenance, as Levinas says, seem to say: "Do not allow me to die." His presence is the most important aspect of the narration; everything revolves around him. It starts from the side of the road, where the person stands vexed and "half dead," avoided by some and taken into consideration by another; one needs to read the entire text and, perhaps, also our own lives, starting from the cruelty and injustice of his condition. The road can be the perfect image of this life of every day, of that era, and of today. The way is long by which we continually come across the others, persons known and unknown. When dealing with the poor—and those marginalized for various reasons—many adopt the attitude of the priest and the Levite, but there are also those who behave like the Samaritan: they abandon their path to draw near.

The account invites us to change direction, to take up all that is implied in leading a life that is truly human and characteristic of a believer. But there is still more: the parable makes us understand that one needs to go beyond one's fellow countrymen, beyond those close to one for ethnic, cultural, or religious reasons, to care for the needy, regardless of their social or religious conditions, for no one is excluded. This is a universality that challenges us, that goes beyond stagnant behaviors but that, at the same time, notices the priority of those who suffer marginalization and injustices.

The neighbor is not the person that we encounter along our paths or on our road, but the one to whom we go out toward for an encounter, to the extent that we abandon our pathway and enter onto that of the other, into his world. It has to do with giving to one's neighbor who is far away, one who is not found in our geographical, social, or cultural sphere. To be exact, we can say that we do *not have* neighbors: we *make* them, through initiatives, gestures, and tasks that make us closer to those who are far off. The neighbor is one who "shows himself" as such: in fact, here we need to translate the verb *gegonemai* (Lk 10:36). Drawing close to the other allows for a double effect: we become neighbors and the other becomes our neighbor; it is a journey of departure and return. Nearness implies reciprocity and is born when we recognize the human dignity of someone, his being our equal and our sister or brother. Hence, Levinas calls nearness "accepted otherness."

What motivates the Samaritan is compassion—in the original sense of suffering with the other—that proves itself in seeing the injured one; Luke expresses it with great clarity by saying that the Samaritan "was moved with compassion at the sight" (Lk 10:33). In the Greek text, this "compassion" is expressed even more dramatically and strongly: *splanchnisteis*—"his innards were moved"—a formulation that reprises a refined point of the original Hebrew.

This deals with a profoundly human sentiment that manifests a great sensitivity—so much so as sometimes to bring about physical consequences—in the face of the pain of the injured person; affirming him means making one understand that, in an evangelical perspective, the religious element is profoundly anchored in the human element. Without an affective nearness, without friendship with the poor and the marginalized, there is no solidarity with him. In the matter at hand, precisely because the Samaritan took upon himself the sorrowful situation of the mistreated person, was he capable of acting correctly.[105]

The parable speaks to us of a "nearness" that encompasses the connotations of welcoming or hospitality, an intense and frequent theme in Scripture. The Samaritan abandoning his road, his world, enters into the life of the wounded one, a stranger, the other. He becomes his host since, in his turn, he welcomes him into his life: a gesture that is prolonged by entrusting him to the care of the innkeeper, making him a participant in his own welcoming. Hospitality also presupposes reciprocity.[106] Hospitality does not cause the disappearance of the personality of the one who is welcomed as a guest into our world, but rather implies respecting it in its otherness and enriching itself with it. The God of the Bible dwells in our history, he is Emmanuel and, in this same movement, he makes us guests of his Kingdom. The Christian community, the Church, gives and receives his presence in the world, and the Council often reiterates this concept.

The parable of the Samaritan highlights the supremacy of the other in the comportment of one who follows Jesus: being a disciple means acting and loving like him: "This is my commandment: love one another as I love you" (Jn 15:12). Acting like the Samaritan means becoming the neighbor of the one who suffers and is marginalized. Let us not forget, moreover, that the Samaritan did not only have compassion, but he practiced mercy; the last word of Jesus to the scribe—and, by means of him, to us—is: "Go and do likewise" (Lk 10:37). He is sent on a mission, that equates to saying, "Give life, practice mercy"—without compromises—in the best and most original sense of the term: putting his own heart, by means of concrete gestures, into the care of the miserable, the defenseless. This is also the case for the disciples of the Lord, taken as one, the Church.

The Council invites us to make our own "the old story of the Samaritan," as Pope Paul VI affirms; or to adopt a spirituality, "a walking according to the Spirit" (see Rom 8:5). This is the witness of Oscar Romero and of many others in these last decades, and it is precisely to this that Pope Francis is calling us, emphasizing the central theme of mercy. It is in this sphere that the Aparecida Conference is situated when it speaks of a Samaritan Church.

A Samaritan Church

The model of spirituality that inspires the parable of the Samaritan highlights the service that the Church, the People of God, must give to humanity, recalling, in particular, the least of society. The story of the Samaritan presents a path that every Christian, and the Church as a whole, must assume. It deals with the disposition to put into practice solidarity in an encounter with needy persons, wherever they might be. It is necessary likewise to be able to depart from one's own path, as the Samaritan did. Pope Paul VI says it very clearly. Having offered some considerations on the Council, he in fact affirms: "All this rich teaching is channeled in one direction, the service of mankind, of every condition, in every weakness and need" (*Discourse*, no. 13). In his discourse opening the second conciliar session, the pope reiterates, moreover: "Let the world know," that the Church "is motivated by the sincere desire not to dominate but to serve" (no. 8).

During the conciliar years, there was insistent talk about a poor and serving Church. Despite this, as we have already observed, the theme of the Church of the poor, in the final documents of the Council, does not have the presence desired by a good number of persons who played a role in this assembly. The attention of the conciliar majority is concentrated, above all, on the other two intuitions of St. John XXIII: the presence of the Church in the contemporary world and ecumenical dialogue, expressing, in these spheres, points of view that are extremely interesting and fruitful. On the contrary, the relationship between the Gospel and poverty, between the proclamation of the Kingdom and the poor, although not having had a great echo in the Council, was taken up again by Medellín, which wished to adopt the proposal of St. John XXIII about poverty as the pivot for the Church's works, precisely on the pastoral and theological challenge which the topic makes.

Putting into practice this evangelical demand has had a series of vicissitudes, of going and coming, of sustenance and resistance: however, it has never been absent from the life of the Church on our Continent. Although it is not present in due dimensions, nor always starting with the instances in which we could expect it, we cannot say, however, that, in the poor countries especially—inasmuch as proposed by the conciliar event and by other important texts on solidarity in relation to the marginalized—for various reasons, it was not strongly present in these years.

Despite this, there is still much to be done. The path traveled is confirmed and sustained today by the decisive word of Pope Francis who wants "a Church which is poor and for the poor" (*Evangelii Gaudium*, no. 198).

It is to this service that the preferential option for the poor tends, a proposal and task whose roots are deeply founded in Scripture and which recognizes as its contemporary sources what is born from the suffering and exclusion in which the poor live, without forgetting the words of St. John XXIII, pronounced a month before the Council: "Before the underdeveloped countries, the Church is present as she is, and as she wishes to be, as the Church of all, and particularly the Church of the poor" (September 11, 1962). Universality and preference of the love of God addresses itself to every person without exceptions and, at the same time, affirms the primary place of the marginalized and of the oppressed in a Christian vision Fidelity to the witness of Jesus means having two contemporaneous dimensions, which feed off one another and which are reciprocally conditioned.[107]

The Conference of the Episcopate of Aparecida (Brazil, 2007) adopted a clear position with respect to the points we are treating. It insisted on the Christological understanding of the preferential option for the poor,[108] making the Samaritan an emblematic figure for expressing the task of the evangelization and humanization of the Church. The Conference affirms: "In the light of Christ, suffering, injustice, and the cross challenge us to live as a Samaritan church (cf. Lk 10: 25-37)," or, in other words, at the service of the least and of the forgotten. It continues with the Lucan text as a guide, "recalling that 'evangelization has always developed alongside the promotion of the human person and authentic Christian liberation'" (ibid.). Bearing witness to the Gospel means sharing the joy of the presence of the love of God in our lives.[109] This is the Good News of the gratuitous love of God that seeks to be engaged in the promotion of justice, in liberation from every type of oppression, and in communion with the God of life. It deals with love for God and for one's neighbor, which constitutes one single reality. Naturally, we are speaking of gratuitous love, not as something arbitrary, but in the sense of its not being motivated by ethical and human merits in general, but rather by its mere existence and necessity, as in the case of the wounded man of the parable dealt with above. It is in this context that the assertion of John is situated: God "first loved us" (1 Jn 4:19); it is he who takes the initiative.

This approach gives solidity to Aparecida's conclusions, and it insists on this aspect in many other places. In harmony with Pope Paul VI, it affirms that responding to Jesus who calls us to follow in his footsteps "requires entering into the dynamic of the Good Samaritan (cf. Lk 10:29-37), who gives us the imperative of becoming neighbors, especially to those who suffer, and bringing about a society where no one is excluded, following the practice of Jesus" (no. 135).[110] "Becoming neighbors" means taking the initiative to draw close to the other, as we saw in the parable, or as Pope Benedict XVI noted, "we must go out to meet the needs of the poor and those who suffer and create 'just structures' which 'are a condition without which a just order in society is not possible'" (*Discourse at Aparecida*, no. 4), so that our Continent would be "our common house" (A., no. 537). In another place, regarding the task of evangelization and the preferential option for the poor, Aparecida speaks of "passionate love for Christ who accompanies the People of God in the mission of inculturating the gospel in history, ardent and tireless in its Samaritan charity" (no. 491). This Samaritan charity is the soul of the spirituality that the Council proposes, a love that must confer strength and depth on the realization of justice and with respect to the human dignity of every person.

The expression "Samaritan Church" is not only evocative, but emphasizes, as well, the courses to be followed in order to proclaim the initial presence of the Kingdom of God in history. Starting with Medellín and inspired by the Second Vatican Council, many on the Continent have adopted this attitude. It is understood that the proclamation of the Good News, addressed to every person, leads to primary solidarity with the poor and the oppressed, rejecting the situation of injustice in which they live, since it is contrary to the plan of the God who is love. This process overflows into the practice of the People of God that, gathered in the conclusions of the Aparecida Conference, acquires a new thrust and opens itself up to new perspectives.

The supremacy of the other—and no one represents this condition more clearly than the poor and the marginalized—is a crucial element of the liberating word of the Gospel. The strong option for the forgotten and the mistreated implies being on his path, making him our guest, seeing him not only as needy or a victim, but also as an equal, no matter how different he might be. In full respect for his right to be an agent of his own history, making our own his vindications for justice and his aspiration for a more human life, we follow the admonition of St. Paul: "Welcome one another, then, as Christ welcomed you, for the glory of God" (Rom 15:7). In fact, the ultimate foundation and decisive reference for the conduct of the Christian is the *sequela* of Jesus.[111]

Starting from the world of the poor, advancing to draw near to the other without making detours to avoid finding oneself face to face with the injustice and suffering that the poor undergo, we can understand the different dimensions of the preferential option for the poor: spiritual, theological, and evangelizing. Living them, in their complexity and repetition, presumes what the Gospel calls a conversion, a *metanoia*; in the Bible, that means abandoning one road and taking another one. In this case, it is the way, and the world, of the poor, with all its complexity and its demand for fidelity to the word of Jesus. This is the point of departure and the indispensable condition for accepting the Kingdom of God and for walking in the footsteps of Jesus, the Christ, who proclaimed the Kingdom and called us to be converted and to believe in the Good News (See Mk 1:15). It is for this reason that the parable of the Good Samaritan has been defined as "a parable of conversion."[112]

In the final paragraphs of his discourse, Pope Paul VI makes precise and sets forth the ultimate meaning of the model of spirituality inspired by the story of the Samaritan: in the encounter with the poor and the marginalized, one encounters Jesus: "In everyone we can and must recognize the countenance of Christ (cf. Mt 25:40), the Son of Man, especially when tears and sorrows make it plain to see" (*Discourse*, no. 16). The text of Matthew makes even more evident and eloquent the gesture of the Samaritan in relation to the needy. In this way, the so-called "reduction to the purely human element" that the Council would have used loses significance. The evaluation of history and service to humanity are part of a spirituality that leads toward the God of the Kingdom: "Our humanism becomes Christianity, our Christianity becomes centered on God; in such sort that we may say, to put it differently: a knowledge of man is a prerequisite for a knowledge of God" (ibid.). In this consists the true theocentrism of the Council.

In these affirmations, we perceive a profound significance of what we have defined as "the conciliar event." The Council thus provides a model of conduct, which has lost none of its freshness, from which to draw inspiration: a personal and communal conduct, deeply evangelical, but which remains open and is a source of inspiration. We find ourselves before a spirituality, a "style of life,"[113] toward a path that deserves to be traveled.

II. Poverty: The Challenge of Faith
Josef Sayer

The friendship between Gustavo Gutierrez and Gerhard Ludwig Müller is a friendship that blossomed in the context of the poor. But what relationship can exist between the poor peasants of Peru and the Cardinal Prefect of the Congregation for the Doctrine of the Faith? Who would not marvel in the face of such a strange question? Nevertheless, it is precisely the answer to this question that distinguishes the present Prefect from his predecessors. It is an answer that causes amazement and that is very simple at the same time.

The one who united Gerhard Ludwig Müller to the peasants of Peru is Gustavo Gutierrez. Without Gutierrez and his liberation theology, Müller never would have arrived among the peasants of the Choquecancha, Cachin, Kacllaraccay, Chejani communities and so many others in the remote Andes mountains of Cuzco, Ayaviri, Puno, Juli, or Huaraz. Without him and his liberation theology, Müller never would have arrived in the poor quarters of Lima, La Paz, or São Paolo. Never would he have dived in such a coherent and lasting way into the difficult life of the peasants: a life of extreme misery between 3,000 and 4,300 meters above sea level, where drinking water is found only in streams, toilets do not exist, and the diet—based only on corn and potatoes—is not balanced; where the possibility of having access to sanitation worthy of the name does not exist; where there is no electricity and where, in the most remote villages, there perhaps exist two grades of primary school, after which one's scholastic education is considered finished. The intuitions of liberation theology as developed by Gutierrez moved the professor of dogmatic theology at the University of Munich to spend up to two months of vacation in an intense sharing of this life, in conditions of extreme misery. This was an eye-opening experience for a professor who came from Germany, and who immersed himself in the culture and in the faith in God of the peasants and of the inhabitants of the poor neighborhoods of the metropolises.

Müller thus experienced that, in order to comprehend the reality of the poor, it is not enough to study books or to evaluate statistics on the poor and, more generally, on poverty. To understand better the Gospel and Jesus Christ himself, Müller descended with coherence into the world of the poor. How did he come to this decision?

In the 1980s, the liberation theology of Gutierrez piqued the interest of the professors of theology in the German-speaking countries and, among them, that of G. L. Müller, a young professor of dogmatic theology in Munich. Remarkably, at that time the Congregation for the Doctrine of the Faith was concerned about the liberation theology of Gutierrez. The controversy progressed until the Peruvian Episcopal Conference itself had to go to Rome for a special meeting with the then-Prefect of the Congregation. It must be noted that the debate on liberation theology was not limited exclusively to the Church in Peru. In the Church of Latin America, along with the supporters of Gutierrez, diverse opponents were found within the hierarchy who attacked his theology with vehemence.

In this turbulent context of 1988, G. L. Müller participated in a research seminar for five weeks for teachers of liberation theology, in Peru. The planning and organization of the seminar were entrusted to Albert Biesinger and Thomas Schreijäck, both then at Salzburg, and to me, a pastor at that time of a community in a poor neighborhood of Lima. Due to my long pastoral experience in the Andes regions of Peru and to my friendship with Gustavo Gutierrez, we were able to convince Müller and many "teams" involved in pastoral work to participate in the research seminar. Following the classic method of the General Episcopal Conferences of Latin America and of Latin American theology—"seeing-judging-acting,"—we began with fourteen days of sharing, in twos or threes, in the communities of peasants in the Andes or in the poor neighborhoods of the big cities. After this, there was a week of reflection: experiences had in different places, where we were assembling and sharing, were made the object of reflection from a theological point of view. These were experiences born from a sharing of the conditions of the life of the poor, linked to pastoral work in different sectors and to social conditions marked by structural and political violence—above all by the violence of what then was called "the dirty war"—and also what we saw in action with the Marxist-Maoist terrorists of Sendero Luminoso and the terrorism of the State, with its reaction no less brutal toward the poor.

After this period of very intense preparation, there followed a week of theological reflection with Gustavo Gutierrez. From today's perspective, this research seminar was one of the most surprising theological events: seventeen German-speaking theology teachers had the possibility to participate every day in a week of presentations by the liberation theologian Gutierrez—who, it should be noted, was not even a professor at the University—and to have discussions with him: a unique situation in which to learn, to teach, and to understand.

This week with Gutierrez greatly struck Müller, and made such an impression as to give birth to the beginning of a long friendship. Moreover, he remained struck by the extraordinary quality of the liberation theology of Gutierrez. From this experience, Müller understood that liberation theology is not limited to a theological and theoretical discussion. Liberation theology concretely addresses the hard life of the poor and the causes that bring about poverty. All this must be considered in the light of faith. In this sense, the poor are not simply the object of theological reflection. The results of theological reflection on the concrete life and situation of poverty are brought into the very life of a community and made the object of reflection together with it. In this theological circle—reflection-praxis-reflection—one also arrives at a fundamental reality for the Christian, as we learned from Gutierrez. According to his spirituality of liberation theology, to become followers and disciples of Christ, one needs to be capable of making one's own the world of the poor and to enter into friendship with the poor themselves. This includes a new quality of theology.

What struck us in a particular way was that Gutierrez was preserving liberation theology from a romanticization of poverty. Poverty does not do good. On the contrary, poverty, in so many extreme and difficult situations of emergency, is the cause of conflicts in families, groups, and communities. The poor are not better than other people. In the interpretation of the option for the poor, Gutierrez insists on the fact that they are the preferred of God, not because *they* are good, but because *God* is good. *God gives his love gratuitously*, above all to one who is denied a life worthy of being lived.

A fact unknown to most is that, as already said, Gutierrez did not occupy any chair of theology in any university. He studied theology in different universities of Europe and therefore had a great familiarity with European theology and, above all, with the events of the Second Vatican Council. He developed his specific theological approach starting from his pastoral work and subsequent reflection on the Peruvian and Latin American context of the 1970s and 1980s and in relation to the General Conferences of Latin American Bishops at Medellín and Puebla. He formulated the name "liberation theology" in 1968, when he was invited for a lecture on the theme "Theology of Development." Gutierrez was convinced that, starting with the social reality of Latin America and with the precarious living conditions of the poor, which includes the majority of the population of the "Catholic" continent, one could not speak of development, so much in vogue during this period. According to the mind of Jesus Christ and his Gospel, in the Latin American situation, it was necessary rather to speak of "liberation" and to ask the fundamental question: how can one speak to the poor of the love of God when they are faced with misery and injustice? Gutierrez developed basic concepts of that relationship in his book, *Teología de la Liberación* (1971),[114] which would become the trademark of an entire theological movement.

The participants in the research seminar during the preparatory meetings, for two semesters before the trip to Peru, already had, among other things, the possibility of reading and debating the Gutierrez book. The lectures of Gutierrez and the discussions with him did not bring us only to what was then the current *status quaestionis*: among ourselves we were also asking how it was possible to get to the point of raising objections against Gutierrez and his theology. In our discussions, we arrived at the conclusion that for many, above all in the spheres of the Latin American hierarchy, this did not involve a theological discussion or a desire to clarify some theological problems. It appeared to us, rather, that liberation theology had been used at the level of ecclesiastical politics and in personal positions in the tense climate of that period, on account of the conflict between the Eastern and Western parts of the world. Clearly, geopolitical conflicts cannot be hidden. Let us take as an example the so-called "Documento de Santa Fe," commissioned by the president of the United States, Ronald Reagan, who, in 1980, arrived at the conclusion that liberation theology and the "Latin American Church" not only must be attentively observed, but also actively combated, because it was contrary to the interests of the foreign policy of the United States in Latin America: this also demonstrates clearly the political background of the discussion about liberation theology.

The debate within the Church was also present at the General Conference of the Latin American Episcopate at Puebla. Gustavo Gutierrez took part in this Conference and was particularly active in the redaction of the texts that dealt with the option for the poor. It is precisely in the option for the poor that Gutierrez sees the heart of liberation theology and of a Church in Latin America that was trying to put into practice the Second Vatican Council and to give a response to the desire of St. John XXIII for a "Church of the poor."

This theology of Gutierrez, liberating theology in the Gospel sense, was situated and rooted in the practice of pastoral care in a community in a poor neighborhood of Lima, where he was working as a pastor. The struggle of the families for daily survival and against "premature" death, particularly that of the smallest babies, as well as the effects of the structural injustice and violence, which St. John Paul II would later define as "structural sin," influenced the theology of Gutierrez. His insistence on "death before its time" matured through his study of colonial history and the theology of Bartolomé de las Casas. In the rereading of the Gospel of Jesus Christ, from concrete social experience in a colonial situation and from the remembrance of the God of the Bible, Las Casas reaches his prophetic accusation of the cruelty of the Conquest that meant a "premature death" for innumerable indigenous persons.[115] The liberation theology of Gutierrez, often thought of superficially, is not therefore revolutionary violence, influenced for example by the Fuochista ideology of the 1970s, or by the Cuban revolution, or by the Sandanistas. Gutierrez speaks of the proclamation of *the God of life*; of a dignified life for everyone, inasmuch as we all are children of God. For this reason, he was also concerned with the history of colonial oppression and of its consequences up to our time. His theology, like that of Las Casas and other theologians, finds its foundation in *the liberating action of God in the Bible*.

Gutierrez, who does not belong to a certain superior white race and who himself has indigenous roots, was sensitive to the racism that existed in Peruvian society in regard to the indigenous peoples, above all in the Andes and in the Amazon. Their marginalization and that of the poor on the outskirts of the big cities were his principal concern. As Gutierrez never tired of repeating, the poor are the "insignificant" of a society marked by a neoliberal economy. The poor are not even used, they are "trash," "garbage," as Cardinal Bergoglio said at Aparecida and which was later repeated by him as Pope Francis. Gutierrez, in his lectures, has always recalled the social encyclicals of the popes. We have learned how these encyclicals play an important role in Latin America and in liberation theology, above all as regards what transpires in Germany where, unlike in Rome, these matters are hardly taken into consideration.

It is obvious that G. L. Müller himself would take these matters seriously since he comes from a family of workers: his father worked on an assembly line of Opel. His family knew the misery and privations of the postwar era. Bishop Ketteler and his engagement on behalf of the poor were part of the formation of the Mainz clergy.

The history of his family certainly facilitated Müller's complete involvement in the situation of the peasants of the Andes. What struck Müller in a particular way was that he shared the simple life of the peasants in the isolated villages of my Andes parish of Lares—where I was then working during the university's holiday season—and not only because the rectory was very rustic and spartan. During his pastoral visits, Müller slept on the earthen floor in the poor clay houses of the peasants on an alpaca rug, having to put up with the annoying presence of fleas and the little pigs of India. He had to walk on foot on steep mountain paths to the villages that were located at 4,300 meters above sea level, facing the cold and hail. He ate with the peasants, usually potato soup and boiled corn. Meat was rarely eaten; the peasants of that region eat meat only eight times a year, especially during the cultivation of the fields, sowing time, the harvest, and on feasts.

Müller also knew the "*faena*," the unpaid communal work to better the situation of the village, as well as other elements of the unique culture of the peasants. He celebrated with them their feasts and he learned to appreciate their capacity for happiness and their popular religiosity, despite their poverty. The dogmatic professor of Munich became part of the groups of Bibliodramma during the courses for the catechists in the villages, thus also drawing near to the Quechua culture. Taking care of the sick, he shared the suffering of the poorest folk. When an operation in the hospitals of Lima was necessary, he worked to make it possible, something often beyond the reach of the poor: without someone's help, sicknesses often bring a person to a certain death. Müller was able to know directly the effects of the age-old abuse of the little farmers by landowners and of the agrarian politics of the government, concentrated mainly on exportation, to the disadvantage of the little farmers.

Thanks to Gutierrez, he was also able to know the life of St. Turibius of Mongrovejo, the second Bishop of Lima. Contrary to the colonial tradition, this bishop appreciated the Quechua peoples and their Incan culture, and he defended them against any exploitation. He visited these peoples during trips across his immense diocese; he convoked a council in Lima that contributed to the inculturation of the faith, as we would say today. Human nearness to the peasants brought them to draw near to the faith.

In this tradition, also included were not only the pastoral visits—at times extremely difficult in the farthest communities—but also the task of Müller in conducting courses of theology in the seminary of Cuzco. There we had to confront great difficulties due to the low level of academic instruction of the seminarians and to the poor preparation of some teachers, who at times were limited to reading directly from text books. Therefore, we were not able to base ourselves on the lessons that they already had on other topics. Starting with our two topics—he with dogmatic theology and I with pastoral theology—we decided to develop a method of integral theological instruction to help the priesthood candidates have a holistic vision of the strict connection between the contents of the faith and the relation between faith and life: from a biblical, dogmatic, and pastoral perspective, we developed theological themes and guided candidates for the priesthood in the production of hours of catechism lessons and homilies. The professor of Munich succeeded in developing a global project of "Catholic dogmatic theology"—something that no dogmatic theology presently does—later translated into different languages; he was not sure how to teach theology in a Peruvian seminary, but adapted it to the context in a creative way, precisely as he writes in the preface to his dogmatic work: "A characteristic of the unending process of appropriation of the faith in human thought is the tension between the definitive revelation of God in history and every new attempt to translate it into the changing horizons of knowledge and in the various contexts of the recipient of the revelation."[116]

The horizon of Müller's understanding went from Cuzco to all of Surandino and the Great South: the Surandino embraces the dioceses and prelatures of Abancay to Juli on the Lake Titicaca. Here are bishops with great personalities like Luis Vallejos, Luis Dalle, Albert Königsknecht (who survived a Nazi concentration camp), Luciano Metzinger, Jesus Calderón, Alban Quin, and Elio Perez, who created, in the spirit of the Second Vatican Council, a *communio* of the local churches. Together, sustained also by the numerous visits and conferences of Gustavo Gutierrez in Surandino, they developed an inculturated evangelization, which united faith and life according to the spirit of Medellín and Puebla. They defended the peasants abused by structural and political violence and, for this critical and prophetic work of theirs, they were certainly not loved by the political authorities. Müller learned to know and to appreciate this form of evangelization and this way of living the Church. He defended these bishops against the new generation of bishops who sought to discredit them with the assertion that they were only capable of a facile "horizontalism" and "sociologism," and that the true evangelization began rather with this new generation. This means that Müller also knows well the difficult controversies of this type within the Church, directly linked to liberation theology and to Gustavo Gutierrez himself.

The fact that Müller was appreciated by the other generation of bishops has a very simple explanation: in the context of a seminar of the theology faculty of the University of Frieburg (Switzerland) on inculturation held in the Grand Sur, which is in the Andes regions of Peru, Bolivia, and Chile, Müller and I were invited by the bishops of this region for a theological consultation near Lake Titicaca.

These theological interventions were later extended to all of Latin America: for example, as a birthday gift for the seventieth birthday of Emilio Stehle, Bishop of Santo Domingo de Los Colorados in Ecuador, we directed the spiritual exercises for his clergy. Bishop Stehle, for his part, thanked us with daily evening stories of his personal experiences with the peace attempts in Central America and of his visit to Fidel Castro in Cuba, where the two discussed theological, social, and political problems for an entire night. As Bishop of Regensberg, and later as Prefect of the Congregation for the Doctrine of the Faith, Müller has continued to be invited for lectures and conferences, for example, by the Brazilian Episcopal Conference, by CELAM in Mexico, and by the Catholic University of Lima. Müller received an honorary doctorate from the Catholic University of Peru, as did Cardinal Joseph Ratzinger, the future Pope Benedict XVI, and Cardinal Rodriguez Maradiaga. Cardinals Rodriguez and Müller both have defended this University from different attacks.

Müller is also interested in international, global questions, especially where problems concern the vulnerability of the poor in spirit and particularly the option for the poor. He has taken part, together with the bishops and cardinals of Africa, Asia, the Pacific region, and Latin America, and with international experts, in a symposium about climate change in the Vatican at the Casa Santa Marta: a symposium organized by Misereor, the work of the German Episcopal Conference for cooperation in development.

Expressing his solidarity with one who suffers was something completely normal for Müller. For example, during a visit to Colombia, those of us who belong to Misereor found ourselves having to guide a delegation of bishops from Europe and from North America. At the invitation of the bishops of the western jungle region of Columbia, we had various discussions at a political level, even with President Uribe, to make clear how acts of violence and the violation of human rights were constantly observed and criticized at the international level. Among other things, we have also visited Bella Vista to recall the massacre of 119 people who were killed in a church. The villagers, all descendants of African slaves, were caught in the midst of guerilla warfare, waged by the army and the paramilitary. Müller also participated in the commemoration of Archbishop Oscar Romero in Salvador, on the occasion of the thirtieth anniversary of his death.

During the research seminar already mentioned, Gustavo Gutierrez always referred to the witnesses to the faith in Latin America and to the extraordinary witness of Oscar Romero. In Salvador, Müller not only participated in the liturgical celebration, but together we visited the "Tutela Legal," an exceptional institution at the residence of the Archbishop of San Salvador, who without fear, like Oscar Romero himself, was committed to fostering respect for human rights during and after the war. The involvement of collaborators of this institution—male and female—is admirable, particularly if we consider how they might be personally exposed to persecutions, even to the point of having their leaders killed. We visited the place where six Jesuits and their housekeepers were assassinated. We have had colloquia with two government ministers and a meeting with the government representative for the cause of human rights.

Now that Müller, as Prefect of the Congregation for the Doctrine of the Faith, has gotten involved in the process of the beatification of Oscar Romero, he can base himself on his intense study of the writings and homilies of Romero, as well as on his knowledge of the social and political context in which Archbishop Oscar Romero worked and lived.

This "Latin American life" of Müller, marked by a friendship with Gustavo Gutierrez, can, on the one hand, seem to be interesting. But in no way has it been an easy path to follow. For Müller, it has meant remaining strong in difficult and uneasy situations, especially while sharing the life of the poor in the Andes of Peru. Passing from an easy life in a big city like Munich to a life without hygienic services, shower, drinkable water, or electricity, is not easy; at the same time, it leads one to become accustomed to a style of life that is very simple and elementary.

On the other hand, his involvement in defense of liberation theology has roused various hostilities against him, some conspicuous and others hidden: hostilities that reached the point of calumny before ecclesiastical authority and even the pope. When in certain periods, many—especially bishops—were avoiding the expression "liberation theology" as the devil avoids holy water, or preferred to bite their tongues rather than pronounce it publically because they thought it inopportune or feared that it would provoke various problems for them, Müller was instead publishing articles on liberation theology, dedicating entire issues to it in the journal, *Münchner Theologischen Zeitschrift*.

To his televised episcopal ordination, he invited Gustavo Gutierrez who, during the concelebration, stood at the altar next to Joseph Ratzinger, then-Prefect of the Congregation for the Doctrine of the Faith. Gustavo very much appreciated this invitation and saw it as a sign of friendship at the very time when in Peru, meanwhile, he found himself receiving visits from various people only at night, like Nicodemus in the Gospel of John.

It is important to note that many attacks against liberation theology and what is at its core—the option for the poor—surfaced from certain groups with a vested interest in Latin America, and Rome found herself having to react to these accusations. The Prefect Joseph Ratzinger was the one who, just before being elected pope, concluded the process of the Cardinal of Lima against Gutierrez. For this, he consulted Gerhard Ludwig Müller. Despite all the tensions, suspicions, and accusations of a presumed lack of orthodoxy, Müller always openly kept his friendship with Gustavo Gutierrez and defended his theology, regardless of whom it pleased or did not. This caused him such hostile relations that certain groups determined to use this issue to seek to impede his nomination as Prefect of the Congregation for the Doctrine of the Faith. However, they failed in their intent, for Pope Benedict XVI focused on the great theological competence of Gerhard Ludwig Müller and named him Prefect in July of 2012.

With Francis, there is now a pope who himself comes from the Church in Latin America and for whom the option for the poor and "the Church of the poor" are central. The General Episcopal Conferences from Puebla up to Aparecida, where then-Cardinal Bergoglio presided over the redaction commission, speaks of the many faces of suffering of the poor in which we recognize the suffering face of Jesus Christ. This also influenced the Christological understanding of Müller. For this reason, he entered quite consciously into the world of the poor. The experiences of Gustavo Gutierrez, as the pastor in a poor neighborhood of Lima, and of Pope Francis, as Cardinal on the outskirts of Buenos Aires, correspond to the experiences of Müller on the outskirts of the countryside of the Peruvian Andes.

The liberation theologian, Gustavo Gutierrez, and the Prefect of the Congregation for the Doctrine of the Faith, Gerhard Ludwig Müller, enjoy a friendship that enriches them personally, as does their shared view of theology, the Church, and the world. It is a friendship that is also fruitful for the Church, which is called to evangelize and to proclaim that redemptive liberation, given us by God through Jesus Christ, is for all: especially and above all for the poor.

Notes

1   G. Gutierrez, *Dove dormiranno i poveri?*, in G. Gutierrez–G. L. Müller, *Dalla parte dei poveri* (Padova: Emi, 2013), 120.

2   See Dogmatic Constitution, *Lumen Gentium*, and *Catechism of the Catholic Church*, no. 721.

3   Pontifical Council for Justice and Peace, *Compendium of the Social Doctrine of the Church* (Vatican City State: Libreria Editrice, 2004).

4   Pastoral Constitution, *Gaudium et Spes*, no.1.

5   Chapter IV, no. 27.

6   See ibid., nos. 27-34.

7   See ibid., no. 29.

8   St. John Paul II, Encyclical Letter, *Sollicitudo Rei Socialis*, no. 32.

9   Ibid., no. 33.

10   St. John Paul II, Encyclical Letter, *Centesimus Annus*, May 1, 1991, on the centenary of *Rerum Novarum*, no. 47.

11   St. John XXIII, Encyclical Letter, *Pacem in Terris*, April 11, 1963, no. 9.

12   Pope Benedict XVI, Encyclical Letter, *Deus Caritas Est*, December 25, 2005, no. 29.

13   St. John Paul II, Encyclical Letter, *Evangelium Vitae*, March 25, 1995.

14   Ibid., no. 2.

15   Ibid., no. 3.

16   The so-called crisis of the hostages of the Japanese embassy began on December 17, 1996, in Lima, Peru. Fourteen members of the Tupac Amaru Revolutionary Movement (MRTA) took as hostages hundreds of high-ranking diplomats, government and military functionaries, and business owners who participated in a feast at the official residence of the Japanese Ambassador in Peru, Morihisha Aoki, during the celebration of the sixty-third birthday of the Emperor Akihito. The crisis was resolved with a blitz that led to the liberation of the hostages and to the death of some of the hostage takers.

17   Cited in *Theologie der Befreiung im Gespräch*, edited by P. Eicher, Kösel. München, 1985, 40-41.

18   Gustavo Gutierrez, *A Theology of Liberation* (Maryknoll, NY: Orbis Books, 1973), 15.

19   *A Theology of Liberation*, 307-308.

20   Congregation for the Doctrine of the Faith, *Instruction on Christian Freedom and Liberation*, March 22, 1986, no. 1.

21   Ibid.

22   Ibid., no. 62.

23   Ibid., no. 65.

24 Ibid., no. 65.

25 See St. John Paul II, Encyclical Letter, *Sollicitudo Rei Socialis*, December 30, 1987.

26 Ibid., no. 81.

27 Augustine of Hippo, *Soliloquies*, I, 2-3.

28 G. Müller, *Dogmatica cattolica* (Milano: San Paolo, Cinisello Balsamo, 1999), 46.

29 See Heb 12:2.

30 See Jn 20:28.

31 See Eph 3:3.

32 See *pantas anthropous*, 1 Tim 2:4.

33 J. Ratzinger, *Truth and Tolerance: Christian Belief and World Religions* (San Francisco: Ignatius Press, 2004), 182-183.

34 Maximus the Confessor, *Mystagogy*, I.

35 See Pope Benedict XVI, Encyclical Letter, *Spe Salvi*, no. 26; Idem., Encyclical Letter, *Deus Caritas Est*, no. 1.

36 See St. Thomas Aquinas, *De rationibus fidei*, 5.

37 G. L. Müller, *Dogmatica Cattolica* (Cinisello Balsamo, Milano: Edizioni San Paolo, 1999), 980.

38 See Rom 5:1-5.

39 See Tertullian, *Apology*, 39, 7.

40 See Gal 3:26.

41 J. Ratzinger, *Introduction to Christianity* (San Francisco: Ignatius Press, 2004), 59.

42 Easter Vigil Homily, April 15, 2006.

43 Pope Benedict XVI, Apostolic Letter, *Porta Fidei*, no. 6.

44 Ibid.

45 Pastoral Constitution, *Gaudium et Spes*, no. 10.

46 R. Spaemann, *Schritte über ans hinaus. Gesammelte Reden und Aufsätze I* (Stuttgart: Klett-Cotta, 2010), 14.

47 Spaemann, Volume II, 9.

48 St. John of the Cross, *Spiritual Canticle*, 23-24.

49 See Eph 4:6.

50 St. Thomas Aquinas, *Summa Theologiae*, I Pars, q. 44, art. 1.

51 See Phil 2:13.

52 Pastoral Constitution, *Gaudium et Spes*, no. 10.

53 See Jn 1:16.

54   Augustine of Hippo, *Sermon 96*, 8.

55   Pope Paul VI, Apostolic Exhortation, *Paterna cum benevolentia*, December 8, 1974.

56   *To Diognetus*, V, 1.4.

57   See M. Nussbaum, *Non per profitto* (Bologna: Il Mulino, 2012), 22.

58   Pope Benedict XVI, Holy Mass celebrated at the conclusion of the encounter with the "Ratzinger Schülerkreis," September 2, 2012.

59   For what follows, the Document of Aparecida will be indicated with the letter "A."

60   This sentence is preceded by the following: "The Church has accordingly often been socially recognized as an entity of trust and credibility. Its effort on behalf of the poorest and its struggle for the dignity of each human being has often led to persecution and even the death of some of its members, whom we regard as witnesses of the faith."

61   The document affirms in various places that it situates itself "in continuity with the preceding Conferences," a concept already present in the inaugural discourse of Pope Benedict XVI: "This Fifth General Conference is being celebrated in continuity with the other four that preceded it: in Rio de Janeiro, Medellín, Puebla and Santo Domingo" (no. 2). On like occasions, the text affirms that it adopts again, with renewed rigor, the perspective of seeing, judging and acting, not to mention the preferential option for the poor. It is for this reason that the prefix "re" is very frequent in the document: revitalize, revisit, renew, etc.

62   See for reference the article of Agenor Brighenti, "*Criterios para la lectura del Documento de Aparecida. El pretexto, el contexto y el texto*" (the original Portuguese will be published in the journal *Convergência* of the Conference of the Religious of Brazil).

63   A manifestation of this maturity was insisted on by the episcopates of the greater majority of the countries—despite the doubts of some—in asking, before and during the conference, that, as in preceding cases, there would be a document at the conclusion of the conference.

64   After various versions were developed during the conciliar sessions, the mention of the Matthean text made by St. John XXIII was not adopted.

65   The Constitution, *Gaudium et Spes*, no. 4, a text which we have already cited, speaks of the task of the Church; numbers 11 and 44 repeat it, referring, however, to the People of God.

66   "The text is comprised of three great parts that follow the method of theological-pastoral reflection of 'seeing, judging and acting.' Therefore, it looks at reality with eyes enlightened by faith and with a heart full of love, it proclaims with joy the Gospel of Jesus Christ to enlighten the mind and the way of human life, and it seeks, through a communal discernment open to the breath of the Holy Spirit, to adopt common lines for an action that would be truly missionary, which is the goal of the entire People of God in a permanent state of mission." (*Summary*, no. 3)

67   In the revised version, to this number were added some phrases that reiterate the concept, as we know, of a reading that starts from faith.

68   A. Gardeil, *"Lieux Théologiques,"* in *Dictionnaire de Théologie Catholique*, t. IX, Première Partie (Paris: Librairie Letouzey et Ané, 1926), coll. 712-747.

69   See the article of Victor Fernández, concerning the Notification received by J. Sobrino, *"Los Pobres y la teología en la Notificación sobre las obras de Jon Sobrino"* consulted in *http://www.uca.edu.ar/esp/sec-fteologia/novedades*.

70   The presence of the theme on the signs of the times in *Gaudium et Spes* owes much to his contributions. See his article, *"Les Signes des temps: réflexion théologique"* in Y.M.-J. Congar–M. Peuchmaurd, *L'Église dans le monde de ce temps*, t. II (Paris: Du Cerf, 1967), 205-225.

71   See in this regard G. Gutierrez, *"Benedict XVI y la opción preferencial por el pobre,"* in *Páginas*, no. 205 (June 2007), 6-13.

72   This passage was not included in Aparecida although its content is present in various texts of the Final Document.

73   The phrase "preferential option for the poor," we find eleven times in Aparecida, while the most brief form—"option for the poor"—appears four times. Of these fifteen mentions, eight are found in Chapter 8 that deals with the theme directly. Moreover, to these one must add numerous texts that indicate the same concept with analogous expressions.

74   The authorized Document adds a phrase to this text, "Yet it is neither exclusive nor excluding," to emphasize the meaning of the word "preferential."

75   See Medellin, "Poverty," nos. 4c and 7, Puebla 1145 and 1147 and Santo Domingo 178 and 164.

76   In this regard, it is interesting to observe that a first draft of the message was presented in a single phrase—the preferential option for the poor and for young people. Nevertheless, there were interventions which recalled the biblical and global character, in virtue of its evangelical root, of the option for the poor and the condition of the pastoral direction for the option for young people; it was therefore decided to separate these two affirmations, and the text was redacted as follows: "Therefore, we reinforce our preferential and evangelical option for the poor," and then, "To accompany the youth in their formation and search for identity, vocation and mission, renewing our option for them." This accompaniment certainly is an important pastoral aspect of which the final Document speaks in the context of the Pastoral Care for Young People (see Aparecida [A]., no. 446a).

77   See nos. 65, 402 and 407-430. Here are considered, among others, migrants, itinerants, HIV/AIDS victims, children who are victims of prostitution, those excluded as a result of technological illiteracy, drug addicts, people who are sick with tuberculosis, prisoners confined in inhumane conditions. Likewise mentioned, once again, are indigenous women, Afro-American women—all of whom Aparecida considers with greater attention than the preceding Conferences.

78   See Gustavo Gutierrez, *"Donde está el pobre está Jesucristo"* in *Páginas*, no. 197 (February 2006), 6-22.

79   St. John Paul II, *Novo Millennio Inenunte*, no. 49.

80   See *Novo Millennio Ineunte*, nos. 25 and 28.

81	The text continues: "In our region there are different indigenous, Afro-American, *mestizo*, rural, urban, and peripheral-urban cultures. . . . To this cultural complexity would also have to be added that of the many European immigrants who settled in the countries of our region" (A., no. 56).
82	Aparecida sees the emergence of these sectors as an opportunity for evangelization: "Indigenous people and Afro-Americans are now taking their place in society and the Church. This is a *kairos* for deepening the Church's encounter with these sectors of society who are demanding the full recognition of their individual and collective rights, being taken into account in Catholicism, with their cosmos vision, their values and their particular identities, so as to live a new ecclesial Pentecost" (A., no. 91). See also nos. 88-97 and 529-533.
83	The text continues in this way: "Their social situation is marked by exclusion and poverty. The Church accompanies the indigenous and Afro-Americans as they struggle for their legitimate rights" (A., no. 89). Concerning the presence of indigenous peoples in Aparecida, see the interesting article of Eleazar Lopez, "*Aparecida y los indígenas*," in *Espacio de análisis, reflexión e información en torno al V CELAM, Boletín de Análisis* 10, 1-6.
84	Another text speaks of the necessity to overcome "a chauvinist mindset that ignores the newness of Christianity, in which 'the equal dignity and responsibility of women relative to men' is recognized and proclaimed (*Discourse*, no. 5)" (A., no. 453). Let us notice the transparency of the language utilized.
85	Numbers 43-82 speak of the sociocultural, economic, and sociopolitical situations.
86	See a brief description of this process in Gustavo Gutierrez, "*Pobreza y Teología*," in *Páginas*, no. 191 (February 2005), 12-28.
87	Various participants in the Conference opportunely requested, as seen in some texts of the Aparecida Document, the elimination of the "and" in the expression "disciples and missionaries," so as to underscore that every disciple of Jesus is necessarily a missionary. The witness of a disciple is, effectively, an indispensable prolongation in the community of the primary missions of the Son and of the Spirit (see *Ad Gentes*, nos. 3-5).
88	The text that follows has already been cited and speaks of the poor as ministers of their own destiny.
89	Aparecida takes up again the idea, alluding to the behavior of the Samaritan who abandons his path in order to care for the injured man: "In the light of Christ, suffering, injustice, and the cross challenge us to live as Samaritan church (see Lk 10: 25-37)" (A., no. 26).
90	"Taking on this option for the poor with new energy, we state that any evangelization process entails human promotion and authentic liberation, 'without which a just order in society is not possible' (*Discourse*, no. 4)" (A., no. 399).
91	Along this same line are the insistence of Pope Benedict XVI and of Aparecida in reiterating that "the Christian life is not expressed solely in personal virtues, but also in social and political virtues" (*Discourse*, no. 3 and A., no. 505).
92	Among the modifications to the final Aparecida text—more numerous than in the preceding Conferences—the most extensive correspond—surprisingly—to the paragraphs that concern the base communities.

93   As Carlos Galli says, Aparecida "was an event, which with the passage of time
       and whose ecclesial reception and real influence, will determine if it reaches
       the level of the 'historic'" ("*Aparecida un nuevo Pentecostés en América Latina y
       el Caribe?*" in *Criterio*, Año LXXX, no. 2328 [July 2007]), 362-371.

94   The text is based on Gustavo Gutierrez, "*Die Spiritualität des Konzilsereignisses*,"
       in M. Delgado-M.Sievernich (Hgg.), *Die Grossen Metaphern des Zweiten Vati-
       kanischen Konzils. Ihre Bedeutung fur heute* (Freiburg: Herder, 2013), 405-421.

95   Medellín (*Introduction*, no. 2) speaks of lights and shadows and later on so too
       did the Roman Synod of 1985, commemorating the twentieth anniversary of
       the closing of the Council (*Final Document*, no. 3).

96   Angelina and Giuseppe Alberigo are right when they say, "Working on John
       was the intoxicating impression of making the history of the future" (*Givoanni
       XXIII—Profezia nella fedeltá* [Brescia: Queriniana, 1978], 108).

97   The best interpretation of the origin of this expression tends, in fact, to the
       way inasmuch as it is the sequela of Jesus; see D. Marguerat, *Les Actes des
       Apôtres 1-12* (Genève: *Labor et Fides*, 2007, 326-327); and P. Mallen, *The
       Reading and the Transformation of Isaiah in Luke-Acts* (London-New York: T & T
       Clark International, 2008), 72.

98   St. John XXIII, Apostolic Constitution, *Humanae Salutis*, December 25, 1961,
       no. 4.

99   Although in another context, we come across in St. John XXIII an early use of
       the expression "signs of the times," appearing in his *Journal of a Soul*, in a text
       written in 1903, which demonstrates his interest in the topic (See A. and G.
       Alberigo, op. cit., 124).

100   On the spirituality of St. John XXIII, see F. Zegarra, "*Juan XXIII: Temas central-
       es de su teología y su espiritualidad*" in *Páginas* 225 (March 2012), 6-14.

101   In the Second Vatican Council, there are two other mentions of "the signs of
       the times." In *Gaudium et Spes*, no. 11, in which it says that the discernment
       must be the work of "the People of God," and in *Presbyterorum Ordinis*, where
       it says that priests "must willingly listen to the laity . . . so that together with
       them they will be able to recognize the signs of the times" (no. 4). See this
       theme in M.D. Chenu, "*Les signes des temps*," in *Gaudium et Spes. L'Église dans
       le monde de ce temps* (Paris: Mame, 1967), 95-116.

102   "But we cannot pass over one important consideration in our analysis of the
       religious meaning of the council: it has been deeply committed to the study of
       the modern world" (Pope Paul VI, *Discourse*, no. 6).

103   The parabolic nature of this passage is discussed since, to be precise, there is
       no point of comparison and because it does not seem to allude to the Kingdom
       of God. In effect, it is unique. Despite this, although the Kingdom is not men-
       tioned explicitly, the witness of the Samaritan with his service to his neighbor,
       to the poor, to the marginalized, proclaims its presence in the daily events of
       human history. Therefore, it can be considered as "an exemplary account," a
       type that is also found in other places in the Gospel of Luke.

104   The positive attitude of Luke toward the Samaritans is well known; see, for
       example, the account of the Samaritan who thanks Jesus for a healing that he
       received in Luke 17:18.

105   This is what Levinas calls "vulnerability": "Only a vulnerable 'I' can love his
       neighbor" (*De Dieu qui vient à l'idée* [Paris: Vrin, 1982], 146).

106   It is significant that the word "guest," designating the welcomed person and
       also the person who welcomes, has the same original Latin root, *hospes*.

107   We recall that the term *preference* is understood with respect to the universality
       of the love of God; in the sphere of this love, there is the inevitable priority
       of solidarity with the poor and the marginalized of society. This, then, is made
       more precise in this way—in the concrete context—that which is intended
       by the term universality. It is wrong, therefore, to remove this word from the
       context of an obvious evangelical exigency and to suppose that it refers to
       a task that one may or may not adopt. It is an option that is part of fidelity
       to the commandment: "Love one another as I love you" (Jn 15:12); a love
       without frontiers and in which "the last will be first, and the first will be last"
       (Mt 20:16). It is an option "that is not optional" (M. Diaz Mateos, "*El grito del
       pobre atraviesa las nubes* [Eccl. 35:21]," *El Rostro de Dios en la historia* [Lima: CEP,
       1996], 146).

108   See Aparecida, no. 392, which takes up and comments on a saying by Pope
       Benedict XVI in this assembly.

109   "Knowing that the Lord loves us, accepting the gratuitous gift of his love is
       the deep source of the joy by which one lives from the Word. Sharing that joy
       is evangelizing. It is the communication of the good news of God's love that
       has changed our life" (G. Gutierrez, "*Praxis de liberación y fe cristiana*," in R.
       Gibellini [ed.], *La nueva frontera de la teología en América Latina* [Salamanca:
       Sígueme, 1977], 13-40).

110   The text continues, noting that this is the Jesus: "who eats with publicans and
       sinners (see Lk 5:29-32), who welcomes the little ones and children (see Mk
       10:13-16), who heals lepers (see Mk 1:40-45), who forgives and frees the sinful
       woman (see Lk 7:36-49; Jn 8:1-11), and who talks with the Samaritan woman
       (see Jn 4:1-26)."

111   The concept is clarified by B. Häring in *The Law of Christ*, which, connecting
       itself to biblical perspectives, renewed moral theology some decades ago.

112   J. Delorame, *Au risque de la parole* (Paris: Seuil, 1991), 231, no. 30.

113   "Christians are characterized by a comportment, by *a style of life*. . . . a manner
       of thinking and acting; in a word, a manner of life" (G. Gutierrez, *Beber en
       su propio pozo*. Lima: CEP–IBC, 1983, 123). It is a way following in the steps
       of Jesus.

114   English translation: *A Theology of Liberation* (Maryknoll, NY: Orbis
       Books, 1973).

115   G. Gutierrez, *Die Historische Macht der Armen* (München-Grünewald-Mainz:
       Kaiser, 1984); Idem., *En busca de los pobres de Jesucristo. El pensamiento de Bar-
       tolomé de las Casas* (Lima: Instituto Bartolomé de las Casas, 1992).

116   G. L. Müller, *Katholische Dogmatik. Für Stadium und Praxis der Theologie*
       (Freiburg im Breisgau: Herder, 1995).